ABOR
TALES
OF AUSTRALIA

ABORIGINAL
TALES
OF AUSTRALIA

A. W. REED

To Julie,

Thought that you could add these to the New Orlean's tales!

Lots of love,

Nic
xx

Reed New Holland

P.S. Might be useful for A level kids - especially transportation assignment thing.

Published in Australia by
Reed New Holland
an imprint of New Holland Publishers (Australia) Pty Ltd
Sydney • Auckland • London • Cape Town

14 Aquatic Drive Frenchs Forest NSW 2086 Australia
218 Lake Road Northcote Auckland New Zealand
86 Edgware Road London W2 2EA United Kingdom
80 McKenzie Street Cape Town 8001 South Africa

First published as *More Aboriginal Stories of Australia* in 1980 by Reed Books Pty Ltd
Reprinted in 1982, 1987, 1988, 1990, 1993, 1994, and 1997
Reprinted in 1998 and 2001 by Reed New Holland

National Library of Australia Cataloguing-in-Publication Data:

Reed, A.W. (Alexander Wyclif), 1908–1979
Aboriginal Tales of Australia.

ISBN 1 87633 418 5

1. Aborigines, Australian—Legends
I. Title.

398.2'0994

Designer: Luisa Laino
Cover illustration and text graphic: Kim Roberts
Typesetter: Midland Typesetters
Printer: Australian Print Group

Contents

Introduction

In recent years there has been increased interest in the Australian Aboriginals, who at one time were regarded as so primitive in their outlook and culture that little purpose was to be served by investigating and preserving their anthropological records. It is only when we are in danger of losing something that we begin to value it, and the large number of books describing the life, customs, arts, and skills of the Aboriginals is ample proof of this renewal of interest.

It is important that white Australians should appreciate the wealth of imagination displayed in Aboriginal legend. It is part of the literature of Australia. We shall not put our roots down into the soil until we have incorporated their folklore into the indigenous literature of the southern continent, and can see the land through the eyes of the primitive, clever, imaginative people who had to fight to gain their nourishment from Mother Earth. It is remarkable that in an environment of desert wastes and infertile soil, as well as in well-watered country, the imagination of the Aboriginals should produce tales that are both beautiful and amusing, and that they should find human characteristics and poetry in bird and beast, in the sky above them, in sun, moon, and stars, and even in reptiles and insects.

They lived close to the soil, these children of nature. They were dependent on her for sustenance, and in the teeming animal life and in the barren places alike they found evidence of the work of a Creator Spirit, and promise of Bullima, the after-life, where game abounded, there was soft grass to lie on, refreshing streams, and soft breezes. From their physical needs a majestic conception of nature was evolved, with beneficent spirit ancestors—and the corresponding spirits of evil that are inimical to mankind.

The legends contained in this book have been gathered from many different sources. It is a comprehensive collection which originated among different tribes and can be regarded as a typical sampling of the beliefs of Aboriginals in every part of Australia.

Coming from widely divergent sources, it is natural that there should be inconsistencies and contradictory elements. This is particularly the case in the Creation myths and the folklore concerning animals when the land was still in the Dreamtime. From some legends we learn that animals and insects were brought to life at the touch of Yhi, the Sun Goddess, and that Man, the final creation, was made in the bodily and mental form of Baiame, the Great Spirit.

Other widespread legends say that all living things first took the form of men, and gradually achieved individual characteristics as animals. This is a reasonable explanation of the origin of totemism, which exercised a considerable influence on Aboriginal life. It is a vast subject, especially as totemism took different forms in various parts of the country. The presentation of myths and legends in a form which is acceptable to the present day must necessarily depart from the spirit of the Eternal Dreamtime in many respects. To the Aboriginal the stories were not simply pleasant tales to beguile the evening hours. As Professor A. P. Elkin remarked, 'Mythology is not just a matter of words and records, but of action and life, for the cult societies, the totemic lodges, do not spend their time at meetings reciting and chanting only; they also re-enact myths, and do so because the heroes and ancestors were, in their belief, actual persons and totemic beings; what they did in the course of their labours must now be done in ritual and the places associated with them must be visited and cared for. For the most part, the details of any myth are only important because they enable the present-day men to walk the path with fidelity, which leads into the sacred dreamtime, the source of life.'*

So far as possible, continuity of theme runs through the collection, but because of the widespread origin of the tales, the reader should consider each legend as a self-contained narrative, without attempting to put it in the context of other stories in the same chapter. For this reason animals sometimes appear as men, and at other times in their natural form. Similarly

---

* *The Australian Aborigines*, A. P. Elkin, Angus & Robertson, 4th edn. 1964, p. 244.

there are several conceptions of the Father-God, the Great Spirit, Baiame. In some he is Culture hero, father and creator of his people, towards whom created man aspires; in others he is a great wirinun, plagued by faithless and foolish wives.

The value of this compilation may well lie in its representative nature. With hundreds of tribes and hundreds of languages, there was no homogeneity of nomenclature, but there was a common ethos which can be readily found by sampling the variant legends of different tribes.

An arbitrary selection of Aboriginal names for living creatures has been made and adhered to throughout in order to avoid confusion, but it will be appreciated that such names varied according to tribe and locality. A glossary of names and Aboriginal terms is given in an appendix.

Many books have been used freely as source material, but variant accounts have been compared and the tales rewritten in a form that it is hoped will appeal to readers of the present time. The modern version of Mrs Langloh Parker's books of Eulalie tradition, edited by H. Drake-Brockman and published by Angus and Robertson in 1953, are particularly valuable. *Myths and Legends of the Australian Aboriginals* by Dr W. Ramsay Smith and published by George G. Harrap & Co. in 1930 is the largest collection previously published.

A. W. Reed

Part I

Legends of the Birds

 Baiame and the Crow

Wahn was the most famous of all the men of the Dreamtime. He was clever and could mimic the cries of animals and birds. After he became fully grown he grew lazy and conceited, expecting other people to work for him while he rested in the shade and amused the women of the tribe or played tricks on his friends. The other hunters became impatient with him and finally drove him away from their camp.

Wahn gathered up his belongings. He placed some food in his dilly bag, a rope of hair, a firestick, and a magic kangaroo bone. Taking his spears and a throwing stick which had not been used for many moons, he journeyed a long way until he came to a water hole beside some tall gum trees. It was a perfect place for a camp. He built two long rows of miamias with branches, and thatched them over with grass. Late one afternoon he lit a fire and climbed into the branches of one of the gum trees. As darkness fell he watched the hunters going back to their own tribes. Some of them looked curiously at the new camp with the many miamias.

When it was nearly dark a lonely hunter who was carrying a wallaby on his back was attracted to the fire. Wahn slipped down the tree, entered one of the huts, and began to cry like a baby. He peeped through the cracks and smiled when he saw the hunter standing still to listen. He flitted from one miamia to another, making a different sound in each: in one, the noise of husband and wife quarrelling; in another, of water boiling in a pot; in another, running water; in another, the notes of birds; and in the last hut, the plaintive song of a young woman singing to her lover.

Neilyeri, the hunter, stood in the doorway of this last hut, looking for the girl whose voice had so enchanted him. Wahn came out of the miamia.

'What are you looking for?' he asked innocently.

'I heard a girl singing.'

Wahn looked at him sideways. 'There is no girl here.'

'But I heard the sound of many people, and a girl singing.'

'I tell you there is no one here. See for yourself.'

The two men looked in every miamia. They were all empty. Neilyeri scratched his head.

'Why are there so many miamias?' he asked. 'Who made them? Why are they all empty?'

'So many questions!' Wahn laughed. 'I built them myself so that people will have somewhere to sleep when they come to visit me. Why don't you stay here? We can cook the wallaby you are carrying and then go to sleep.'

'No, I am going home,' Neilyeri said hastily. He felt there was something strange about these empty miamias. He ran away, but stopped abruptly when he came to the end of the double row of miamias. Outside the circle of firelight everything was black. There were no stars, and no way to find a path to his own camp.

'Don't worry,' said Wahn, coming up to him and taking the wallaby off his shoulders. 'Come and warm yourself by the fire.'

No sooner had the hunter spread his hands out to warm them than Wahn gave him a push which sent him plunging into the middle of the fire, where he was burnt up till nothing was left save a few charred bones.

'This is the life!' Wahn said as he raked away the ashes and put the wallaby to roast on the hot stones. The meat, together with leaves and roots that he had gathered, lasted him for several days.

After a week had gone by, all the food was exhausted. Wahn lured another hunter into his camp at nightfall, pushed him in the fire, and cooked the meat the hunter had brought with him.

This went on for a long time. Wahn was never discovered, because he was careful to choose hunters who came from different tribes. But one day men gathered together from many different parts of the plain for a corroboree.

'Where is Neilyeri?' someone asked.

No one knew where Neilyeri was, nor the other hunters who had disappeared one by one. It dawned on them that there had been many disappearances, and they began to connect them in their minds.

An old man swayed backwards and forwards as he sat on the ground and crooned,

What shall we do?
Who will be next?
What shall we do?

Others joined in and soon many men were all singing together, 'What shall we do?'

A tall figure strode into the circle.

'What shall we do about what?' he asked with a smile.

Everyone stopped singing and shouted, 'Baiame! It's Baiame!'

And indeed it was Baiame, the Great Spirit, who had been born before time began.

'What can Baiame do to help you?' the Great Spirit asked. 'I have come to you as a man because I knew you needed me.'

He listened to the tale of the hunters who went hunting and never came back. He thought for a while and then said, 'Stay here. I am going away. For a little while you will see no stars at night, but when they shine again you will know that I have gone back to my home in the Milky Way. Then the hunters may leave their camps in the morning knowing that they will return safely at night.'

Suddenly he was gone.

Now Baiame stood alone in the middle of the plain with a wallaby slung over his shoulders. Many tracks led towards a camp where there were two rows of miamias, but there were no footprints leading away from it. He walked slowly towards it and heard the sound of a baby crying, the voices of men and women, the notes of birds, the sound of running water, and lastly the sad song of a young girl mourning for her lover.

Baiame strode out of the gathering darkness into the firelight.

'What are you looking for?' asked Wahn.

'I heard a girl singing.'

Wahn looked at him sideways. 'There is no girl here.'

'But I heard many people, and a girl singing.'

'There is no one here. See for yourself.'

'It doesn't matter,' Baiame said wearily. 'I'm tired. Let me sleep in one of your miamias.'

'Very well,' Wahn said. 'But first come to my fire and warm yourself. Bring your wallaby with you.'

Side by side they walked towards the fire. When they came close, Wahn stepped behind the Great Spirit. Baiame stooped suddenly, caught Wahn by the ankle, swung him round like a churinga on the end of a string, and hurled him into the fire.

The flames leaped high, and Wahn grew smaller and smaller, and sank down into a little heap of ashes. Baiame bent over and blew on them. They swirled and whirled in the flames and fluttered out of the fire and up into the branches of one of the trees.

Baiame looked up. A bird perched on the bough of the tree and cawed at him. The ashes had turned into a bird, a bird who a little while before had been a man mocking the cry of a baby and the song of a young woman, a bird who was now Wahn the Crow, watching Baiame going back to his home in the sky.

 Why the Pelican Is White and Black

Thousands of people were drowned in the great flood of Tiddalick. They were swept away like straws in the raging waters. Some clung to trees, but the water rose so high that they were torn from their refuge.

Only a few men and one woman managed to escape to a hilltop which, when the flood was at its height, became a small island. They watched the water swirling past and wondered whether it might have been better to have met a quick death by drowning instead of dying slowly of starvation.

One morning, to their relief, they saw a canoe in the distance. As it drew closer they could see that it was being paddled by Booran the Pelican.

'Help! Help! Come and help us,' they cried.

'Yes, I will help,' he replied at length, 'but as you can see, my canoe is small. I can take only one of you at a time.'

The woman came forward eagerly, but Booran ordered her back. 'I will take the men first.'

One by one he took them across the lake to the distant shore. When the canoe left with the last of the men, and the woman was left alone on the island, she was frightened. She knew that when Booran returned he would take her for his wife, and she had no desire to marry Pelican.

She covered a log with her possum skin rug, and rolled it near the fire so that it looked as though she were lying asleep on the ground. The flood was receding and the shore was not so far away as when Booran had first arrived. She slipped into the water and swam away in the opposite direction.

Pelican came back and pulled his canoe well up the bank. He fluttered towards the remains of the encampment and chattered excitedly to himself when he espied the sleeping form of the woman wrapped in her rug. There was no finesse in his approach. He went up to her and kicked her in the ribs, and then staggered back in agony as his claws came in contact with the hard wood.

Pelican Booran tore the rug away and realised that he had been duped. His excitement turned to anger. He danced with rage, swore vengeance on the woman and her friends, and daubed himself with white clay in imitation of warriors who paint themselves for the corroboree. Jumping into his canoe, he paddled furiously to the shore of the lake. There was no sign of the men, but along the shore came another black Pelican—one who was much bigger and stronger than Booran.

He looked in astonishment at the white streaks on Booran's black plumage and realised that the strangely marked bird was likely to make trouble. Before Booran could defend himself he rushed forward and impaled him on his beak.

Booran lay lifeless on the shore, his beak pointing pathetically to the sky, his feathers torn and bedraggled and patchy with the white pipeclay. And ever since that day when the flood of Tiddalick receded, the plumage of the Pelicans has been a mixture of black and white.

 ## The Cannibal Cook

There are black Magpies with splashes of white on their tail feathers and wings, and Bell Magpies which have drab, grey plumage. Moograbah was the name of the Bell Magpie, long before he was turned into a bird, while he was still a man.

Moograbah was famous for his cooking. Where others would make an unappetising mess, Moograbah could cook a delectable meal to make any man's mouth water. Cakes that he baked with grass-seed were eagerly sought after, and men came from long distances to barter valuable goods for them. What was not realised for a long time was that the cakes were only a kind of bait for human beings. When visitors came to his camp, he fed them with his cakes until they fell asleep. Then Moograbah crushed their heads with his club and roasted them on the same fire that he had used to cook the grass-seed cakes.

It was only when too many coincidences had occurred that men began to talk. Relatives had been seen going through the bush towards Moograbah's camp, and had never returned. Suspicion crystallised into certainty. A strict watch was kept, and one day the cook was seen devouring his horrible meal. The word spread like fire in the brush. Men gathered together from a distance to discuss such a serious matter.

'It will be better to take him by stealth rather than by numbers,' they decided. 'If we fight him some of us are bound to be killed. Who will volunteer for the task?'

'I will,' said little Gidgeereegah and his big friend Ouyarh. 'We will pretend that we want to eat his cakes, and then we'll take him unawares.'

'You will have to be very careful,' they were told. 'It is not only Moograbah that you have to overcome. He has two wives and two strong sons.'

'We will be careful,' they said, and went away to prepare themselves for their visit. Gidgeereegah painted himself all over with bright green and yellow and red, while Ouyarh tied his yellow hair into a knot. They walked round each other admiringly.

'Moograbah will think we are important visitors,' they told one another. 'He will suspect nothing.'

They took their waddies and spears and went straight to the camp. Bell Magpie saw them coming and went to meet them.

'What do you want?' he asked with a grin.

'We have heard of your famous cakes from many people.'

Moograbah held out his arms as a sign of welcome.

'You have come at the right time. The fire is burning and the grain has been ground.'

He welcomed them into his gunyah and busied himself with his preparations. After a while he carried the hot cakes in to them. Gidgeereegah and Ouyarh ate one or two and hid the others behind them, fearing that they might contain herbs which would put them to sleep.

'Do you like my cakes?' asked Moograbah.

'They are the best cakes we have ever tasted. Now we are sleepy.'

'Lie down then, both of you. I have put kangaroo skins on the floor for you. When you wake up I will have more food ready.'

They closed their eyes and pretended to be asleep. Moograbah came to the entrance with his sons and pointed at them, speaking softly.

'I have never seen such fine-looking men. Look at their beautiful garments, and the splendid topknot on that one! They will make good eating and an ornament to my cooking fire. I will lie down beside them in case they wake up suddenly. When I call you, bring your spears and we shall have a great feast tonight.'

Moograbah lay down and closed his eyes. It was hot in the gunyah and he was drowsy with the heat of the fire. When he began to breathe heavily his two visitors opened their eyes and got cautiously to their feet. They drew back their spears and thrust them through the cannibal's heart.

'Now for the sons,' said Ouyarh. 'Do you remember what Bell Magpie's voice sounded like?'

'I do,' Gidgeereegah said grimly. Imitating the voice of the dead man, he called, 'Come at once. They are dead. I need help.'

The two young men came in, one after the other, and were promptly knocked on the head. The visitors carried them outside, made a pile of dry leaves and twigs, and laid heavy logs over it. The bodies were placed on top.

'There are still the wives,' Ouyarh said. 'They too have eaten human flesh, and must share the fate of their husband and their sons. We must destroy every shoot of this evil tree.'

When the women came home to prepare the evening meal, they were killed and their bodies added to the pile. A burning twig from the cooking fire was applied to the dry leaves. The flames roared up in the dusk, and before the sky was covered with stars the bodies of the cannibal cook, his sons, and his wives, had crumbled to ashes.

The fire died down. Suddenly in the midst of the red embers there was a flapping of wings and a bird, covered in grey ash, rose from the glowing pile and soared upwards, calling its own name, 'Moograbah', as it went.

That was how the grey Bell Magpie came by his drab plumage. Gidgeereegah and Ouyarh were also transformed into birds, but for them it was badge of victory. The colours of their clothes were retained in their feathers: Ouyarh the Cockatoo has a brilliant yellow crest, while Gidgeereegah the Budgerigar, or Warbling Grass Parrot, clad in the soft grey cloak he wore, has patches of colour on his face.

Moograbah still calls to them, hoping they will eat more of his cakes and put themselves at his mercy; but Ouyarh and Gidgeereegah ignore him and go about their own business quietly and peacefully, for their task is ended.

 ## The Fate of Soldier Bird and His Family

The Mullians, or Eagle-hawks, went out to hunt the emus, carrying their net with them. It was five feet high and several hundred yards in length. As they left the camp they saw Deegeenboya the Soldier Bird sitting by himself sharpening the point of his spear.

'Come along with us, Deegeenboya,' they called, because they felt sorry for him. Soldier Bird was old and had great difficulty in getting enough food for his two wives and daughters.

'Thank you,' the old man said in a quavering voice. 'You are kind to spare a thought for me. Don't wait for me—I will come as quickly as I can.'

The Mullians ran on until they came to a place where they knew the emus were nesting. Moving quietly, and without speaking, they thrust long poles into the ground and tied the net to them. It was built with converging arms, with the third side open, and a length of net lying loose in order to close the trap when they were ready.

Leaving two of their number by the net, the others spread out in a wide circle which enclosed the trees where the emus were nesting. There was a gap in the line opposite the open side of the net. When everyone was ready, they rushed forward, shouting at the top of their voices. The startled birds ran out from the trees and fled from the advancing men, straight into the net. As the hunters passed the nests they gathered up the eggs and put them carefully in their bags. When they reached the net, the men who had remained by it had already closed the opening, the six birds were trapped and were running frantically from one side of the enclosure to the other.

They were soon killed, and made into two pies, one small and the other large. The eggs were baked in the ashes of a fire and eaten while the emu flesh steamed slowly in a big earth oven. When it was opened the birds were taken out and a delicious odour of cooked meat rose on the still evening air. Old Deegeenboya, who had arrived shortly before, wiped the saliva from his chin and said to the leader of the Mullians, 'I will help you carry the birds back to camp.'

Mullian-ga put his hands on his hips, threw back his head, and roared with laughter.

'Oh Deegeenboya, your shrivelled shanks would give way before you'd gone half a mile.'

'Please, Mullian-ga. I did nothing to help you catch the emus, but at least I can carry one of the birds home.'

'Very well, we'll let you carry one of them, but you'll have to hurry to keep up with us.'

The young men put the smallest bird on Deegeenboya's back, lifted up the others, and began the long trek back to camp. Deegeenboya was soon left behind, but Mullian-ga went back and appeared suddenly beside him.

'You have done very well, old man,' he said. 'Let me take your burden now.'

'No, no,' Deegeenboya pleaded. 'I don't want to be a burden to you. Even though I am old, it is a challenge to my manhood. If I succeed in carrying it back to camp perhaps you will give me a leg of the bird to feed my family.'

'We will certainly do that,' Mullian-ga said. 'But I warn you that if you are too long we shall have to come back to help you.'

When Mullian-ga had gone on, Deegeenboya permitted himself a crafty grin. Not far away a large stone was lying on the ground, and by its side was the trapdoor that led to the home of Murga-muggai, the Trapdoor Spider, who was a friend of his. He hurried over to it, raised the door, and called down the tunnel, 'Are you there, Murga-muggai? It's me, Deegeenboya.'

'Come in, Deegeenboya. What have you got there?' he asked as Soldier Bird came backwards down the tunnel, dragging the body of the emu after him.

'Murga-muggai, my friend,' he said, panting a little, 'I want you to help me. The Mullians have given this bird to me. I want to get it home before they arrive. If you will let me go down your tunnel I will get there without being seen.'

'You are quite right,' Trapdoor Spider said. 'The other end comes out close to your gunyah, but I don't think you can carry such a heavy load. Let us cut it in half and then it won't weigh so much.'

Deegeenboya sighed. He knew that he would have to give half his treasure to Murga-muggai in payment for using the tunnel.

While Deegeenboya was talking to his friend, Mullian-ga left his companions.

'Take the emus on to the camp,' he said to his men. 'I feel uneasy about Deegeenboya. He is a very old man and he may be in trouble.'

He turned back and searched for Soldier Bird. There was still sufficient light for him to see the old man's trail. It led up to an isolated stone and then disappeared. The trapdoor was half concealed by the stone and he did not notice it.

He ran back to his men and said, 'Something strange is going on. I think Deegeenboya has deceived us. Bring the birds along as fast as you can. I am going on ahead.'

When he arrived at the camp he went straight to Soldier Bird's gunyah and saw Deegeenboya's children climbing a tree. He examined the place carefully and saw the trapdoor at the other end of Murga-muggai's tunnel, close beside the tree. The light dawned in his mind. It was as though a dry piece of wood had flared up among the dull embers of the fire when he saw the trick that the old man was playing on him. The anger in his heart burned as fiercely and clearly as the light that had come to his understanding.

Mullian-ga stood under the tree and called out to the older girl.

'Your father asked me to come ahead to see whether you were all right. What are you doing up there?'

'We are having such fun in the tree,' she replied. 'We were pretending to be birds. We've built a nest up here.'

'You might fall out,' Mullian-ga said. 'Anyway it's time for little girls to go to bed. Jump down and I will catch you in my arms.'

She drew back in alarm. 'It's too far. I might hurt myself. We'll climb down.'

'It's not so very far,' said Mullian-ga. 'It's much more fun to jump. You will really be a bird then, flying through the air. See, I'm waiting to catch you.'

The girl jumped straight at him, but Mullian-ga stepped to one side and she crashed to the ground and lay still. Her little sister began to cry, but Mullian-ga soothed her.

'She will be all right soon,' he said. 'She didn't jump in the right place.'

But the girl continued to sob, holding tightly to the tree. Mullian-ga became impatient and shouted at her so loudly that she was startled. She toppled over, clutched desperately at the leaves, and fell headlong down, bouncing off a lower branch and falling to the ground with a piercing shriek.

Deegeenboya's wives heard the cry and came rushing from the camp to see what had happened to their daughters. Mullian-ga concealed himself behind the tree. As the women came past the gunyah and bent over the bodies of their children, he thrust his spear through their bodies and those of the girls and dragged them all to the foot of the tree.

Then the Eagle-hawk leader sat down to wait, with his eyes fixed on the trapdoor. After a while it trembled and was thrown back. Mullian-ga lifted it clear.

'Thank you,' Deegeenboya said, thinking that one of his wives had come to help him. He climbed out of the tunnel, closed the door, and turned round.

'It was kind of you to bring the bird all this way for us,' Mullian-ga said grimly.

Deegeenboya started.

'I was glad to help,' he said nervously. 'My friend Murga-muggai let me use his tunnel because it was easier to come that way.'

'Very kind of him; but it is the last time you will use it, I promise you. I see that half the bird has vanished already, and by the time you and your family had finished with it, it would have disappeared completely.'

'Oh no, Mullian-ga! We were going to give it back to you, but you did promise that my family could have a little bit. Where are they?'

'Here.'

Mullian-ga showed him the bodies of his wives and daughters.

'There is no place in my camp for thieves. Your family has already paid the penalty. Now it is your turn.'

Deegeenboya's thin legs shook so violently that they could not support his old body. He sank to his knees and begged Mullian-ga to spare his life, but Mullian-ga the Morning Star, the bold leader of all the Mullians, had no pity in his heart for the aged one who had tried to deceive him. His waddy crashed down on the old man's head, and he fell down beside his womenfolk.

There was a bustle and a stir by the camp fire, and an excited chattering as the Mullians brought in the cooked birds. After the feast everyone joined in the dancing and singing. No one spared a thought for the old man or his wives and children who lay stiff and cold beyond the circle of firelight. They had met the punishment that is visited upon all thieves.

 ## Why Cuckoo Has No Nest

Of all the birds that Nungeena the Mother Spirit made, the one with the loveliest voice was Cuckoo. And of all birds, the most conceited was Cuckoo. It was his voice and his vanity that brought about his downfall, and the manner of it was this.

Marmoo the Evil Spirit had tried to destroy Tya, the world that Baiame had beautified, by sending a plague of insects, grubs, and beetles to devour it. Baiame and the friendly spirit Nungeena had thwarted his evil plan by creating birds which ate up the insects.

Marmoo went back to his wife and asked her what he should do next. She gave a wicked chuckle.

'Baiame has given beautiful voices to the birds,' she said. 'They know that you are their enemy, but if you tell them what wonderful songs they sing, they will become your friends.'

'You silly woman,' Marmoo said, 'what good will that do me? I don't want to be their friend. I want to destroy them.'

The woman rubbed her arm where Marmoo had struck her and said resentfully, 'No you don't. You are jealous of Baiame. What you really want is to hurt him. If you will only listen to me, I will tell you what to do.'

'Go on, then,' Marmoo said curtly. 'Tell me.'

'If you praise them and tell them what beautiful voices they have, they will listen. I know. I am a woman. You should tell them how proud Baiame must be. Say that the way to please him is to keep on singing. Tell them that the only thing Baiame wants is to hear them sing.'

Marmoo lifted his hand threateningly. His wife shrank back.

'If you hit me again I won't tell you. Listen, you bad-tempered man. The birds will be so pleased that they will sing all day long. They won't even have time to build their nests. And if they have no nests there will be nowhere to lay their eggs. And if there are no eggs there will be no birds to eat the insects. Now do you see?'

A crafty smile spread over Marmoo's face.

'Trust a woman to think up a good way of doing a bad thing,' he said. 'Yes, my dear, it's worth trying.'

He went to the birds and praised their songs. They listened to him eagerly and nodded their heads in agreement; but when he went on to say that all Baiame wanted was to hear them sing all day long, they laughed at him and said, 'Oh no, Marmoo. You are quite wrong. Baiame loves to hear us sing, but he wants us also to build nests, and make love, and lay eggs, and hatch them, and provide food for our fledglings. Singing is for love-making and joy; but there is work to do as well.'

They flicked their tails and flew away. Only Cuckoo remained.

'You have a voice that is worth all the others put together,' Marmoo said, and Cuckoo believed him.

There are many different kinds of cuckoo in Australia. The one who had listened so intently to the Evil Spirit called all the members of the cuckoo tribe to a meeting with Marmoo.

'There has never been such a chorus of beautiful voices as I can hear today,' Marmoo told them. 'I have heard the songs of birds in the early morning, and at midday, and again in the evening; but they were nothing to compare with yours.'

The cuckoos fell silent, eager to hear more.

'I want you to sing all day long, because then you will help to make Baiame's world a place where men and animals and even spirits can live happily for ever.'

'But we have other things to do beside singing,' said one of the smallest cuckoos. 'There are nests to be built so that we can lay our eggs; and when the eggs are hatched there is no time for singing, because we are busy all day long feeding the young birds. You have no idea how much a fledgling cuckoo eats.'

'Oh yes, I have,' Marmoo replied. 'I want to talk to you about that. You all admire the Great Spirit Baiame and the Mother Spirit Nungeena. Have you ever seen them building nests and feeding their young? Of course not! They are content to leave the hard work to you.'

'That is true,' another cuckoo said. 'Why should we work while they are playing? I think it would be much better if we sang to them. I'm sure it would be much better for them, and they would praise us for giving them so much pleasure.'

In their vanity all the cuckoos agreed, and flew off, singing with full throats and hearts bursting with pride. Marmoo grinned to himself and went back to the other birds to try to persuade them to follow the example of the cuckoos. He failed. They were too busy flying backwards and forwards with grass, moss, feathers, and twigs with which to build their nests.

The night-loving Mopoke had been curled cosily inside a hollow tree. He had been woken by the chatter and song of the cuckoos and had heard what Marmoo had said. As soon as it was dark he flew off to the bower where Baiame lived and warned him that the evil Marmoo was acting suspiciously, and trying to get the birds to do something harmful.

'What it is I don't know,' he said. 'All that he is asking is for them to sing their songs, and that is a pleasant thing to hear. But he has some dark purpose behind it, I know.'

'I know too,' Baiame agreed. 'I know what it is. Summon all the birds here to talk to me.'

The next day a vast flock of birds flew to the mountain and settled round the Great Spirit, anxious to hear what he had to say to them, for they knew he loved them all.

'Is everyone here?' Baiame asked.

'The cuckoos haven't come yet,' Mopoke answered, for he had been peering intently at the gathering throng with his huge eyes.

Presently they all heard the sound of birds singing. The cuckoos arrived in a compact group and sat on the outskirts of the crowd.

'It is you I want to speak to especially,' Baiame called. 'Why were you so long in coming?'

'We were singing,' said the largest cuckoo impudently, singing the words instead of speaking them. 'We are going to spend all our time singing. Why should we build nests and waste the sunny days fetching and carrying and feeding our young and catching silly insects for you?'

'There are many reasons,' Baiame said gravely. 'If all the birds did that there would be no fledglings, and in the end there would be no birds to sing. Work is a good thing. I know. Have I not worked hard to make the world beautiful for you and me? All the work will be undone if you do not eat the insects that are trying to devour Tya, the land of Baiame.'

The cuckoo tossed his head and sang defiantly, 'The cuckoos do not care. The cuckoos will be the singing birds while all the others do your bidding.'

Baiame smiled sadly and said, 'I am sorry for you. Your heads have been turned by pride. Your sweet voices must be taken away from you.'

The cuckoos began to sing louder than ever, but stopped in dismay. Their voices sounded harsh even to themselves. The sound that came from them had become a crazy chorus of croaking and twittering and squeaking. The other birds turned on them and drove them away to the waste lands of the north.

'Don't ever dare to come back to our lovely land,' they cried. 'If you do we will drive you away. Birds that will not work do not deserve to live in Baiame's land. We will see that the insects are kept at bay. We will even feel sorry for you when our children lift their heads out of our nests and we know the joy of mother love and father love.'

Winter passed by. Yarrageh, the Spirit of Spring, blew across the land with her soft breath. In the arid lands of the far north the cuckoos longed for the land of Baiame and the companionship of the other birds. They forgot that they had been warned never to return. They flew to the trees and bushes where the rest of the birds were building nests once more.

The cuckoos laughed to themselves. 'How silly they are to waste their time. They never have any fun. We're much better off, even if we have lost our voices, because it is good to play in the sun all day long and sleep at night.'

Presently the nests were finished and the mother birds sat warming the dainty eggs they had laid. Whenever they flew off to get food the cuckoos would cluster round to admire the delicate white and pink and brown and speckled eggs.

'It is time we laid our eggs,' they said, 'but where can we put them?'

'There are the nests all ready and waiting for you,' whispered a voice. Marmoo the Evil Spirit had returned. 'I am your friend. I've helped you all the time, even though you didn't know it. Go on,' he said to the biggest cuckoo. 'Throw out one of the eggs in this nest and lay yours in its place. The mother bird will never know the difference.'

The biggest cuckoo did what Marmoo had told him. Then they all hid in the leaves of a nearby tree to see what would happen. Presently the mother bird came back. She did not notice that one of the eggs had been changed, and sat down and spread her soft wings over the nest.

'See!' Marmoo whispered again. 'You don't need to look after your young birds. The other birds will do it for you.'

The cuckoos flew out of the tree and laid their eggs in every waiting nest. They felt no love towards their offspring. When the young cuckoos hatched out, they proved to be as selfish and inconsiderate as their parents, demanding more food from their foster-parents than all the other birds in the nest.

It is only because the birds that were loyal to Baiame do not recognise the cuckoos in their nests that they continue to feed them, as they have done for countless generations.

 ## Why Emu Cannot Fly

Dinewan the Emu was the leader of the bird tribe. They all looked up at him because he was large and strong. His huge wings carried him great distances, and his wife had nearly a score of children each year. No wonder that he was feared and respected. And, as was only natural, he had enemies, chief of whom was Goomblegubbon the Bustard or Brush Turkey.

The Brush Turkey was a large bird too, but no one obeyed his orders as they did with Dinewan. He envied Emu's power of flight and the way he could run swiftly across the plain without tiring. Goomblegubbon told no one but his wife that he had determined to do some lasting injury to Dinewan. It took him a long time to perfect a plan that satisfied him. He waited until he knew that Dinewan was going out on the plain to feed, and made sure that he was there well before Emu. He held his wings close to his sides, ruffled up his feathers, and squatted on the ground where the grass was rich and long.

Dinewan alighted nearby and began to browse on the grass.

'Good morning, Dinewan,' Brush Turkey said.

'Morning,' Emu said, barely pausing as he took big beakfuls of grass.

'I have some splendid worms here if you would like them.'

'No. Never eat them.'

'Did you have a good flight out here?'

'M-m-m-m,' said Dinewan, not even stopping eating.

Goomblegubbon waited until Emu had eaten enough and was feeling in a better mood.

'Dinewan, as a friend there's something I would like to say to you. You are so strong and handsome, and everyone admires you so much, that they don't like to say anything to you.'

Emu looked at him curiously.

'It's a strange thing for you to be so concerned with my welfare, Goomblegubbon.'

'I assure you it's for your own good, otherwise I wouldn't dare to address the chief of all the birds.'

'Speak up then,' Dinewan said, a trifle impatiently.

'Well, what I want to say is that I'm surprised that you fly through the air when you want to go anywhere.'

Dinewan looked at him incredulously.

'What on earth and in the sky do you mean, Goomblegubbon? Are you out of your mind? I have the most powerful wings of any bird, better even than Mullian's. How else would I go?'

'Walking.'

'Walking? Like slow, ugly Goanna? Pull yourself together, Goomblegubbon, and talk sense for a change.'

'I am talking sense, Dinewan. Just as I said, no one but a friend would tell you these things. You see, flying is something that any bird can do, even the weakest and commonest ones. Any bird can fly. It's only men, and strong birds like you and me, who are able to get about by walking. It's a sign of distinction to walk. Look!'

He ruffled out his feathers still further, keeping his wings pressed closely to his body and strode quickly round Dinewan on his strong legs.

'See how steadily I go ... how fast I can travel? I've given up using wings altogether. Your legs are longer than mine and much stronger. Imagine Curlew or Cockatoo trying to catch up with you on their tiny legs! That's why they have to fly, but it's scarcely becoming for the great leader of the birds to compete with them in the air.'

Dinewan took a few steps forward and said thoughtfully, 'You may be right, Goomblegubbon. I must talk this over with my wife.'

He spread his wings, and then hastily clapped them to his sides, and began to stride across the plain towards his home. Goomblegubbon laughed as the little cloud of dust grew smaller, and he flew off to tell his wife all about it.

The next day the two birds met again.

'I have followed your advice, Goomblegubbon. I'm sure you are right. My wife and I chopped off our wings with a stone tomahawk last night. It was rather painful, but my leg muscles are growing stronger already. I'll race you to that bush.'

Brush Turkey laughed derisively.

'I never thought you could be deceived so easily, Dinewan. Your brains must be as small as a fledgling's. But if you want to I'll gladly race you to the bush.'

Emu sprinted across the sun-baked ground, the earth coming from his flying feet in little spurts of dust. Goomblegubbon waited until Emu had nearly reached the bush, then spread his wings, and flapped noisily through the air, alighting well ahead of Dinewan. The larger bird stopped suddenly.

'I thought you said it was only common birds who used their wings?' he exclaimed. 'I thought you said you had taken off your wings?'

Goomblegubbon laughed louder than ever.

'What a simpleton you are, Dinewan. I said nothing of the sort. What I did say was that I had given up using my wings. That was yesterday, but today is another day, and tomorrow is another day again. I'm afraid you will have little authority with your people from now on. They will hardly respect a bird who is not a bird, one who is unable to fly. I expect it will be Mullian who will become the new leader—or it might even be me! To be a leader you must have two things you lack: wings, and brains!'

Slowly the truth dawned on Dinewan. He ran forward and struck at Goomblegubbon with his powerful legs. With another gobbling laugh Brush Turkey flapped out of his reach and flew back to his home to tell his wife how he had humiliated the chief of the birds.

A whole year went by. Dinewan never said anything to Goomblegubbon about the loss of his wings, and this puzzled Brush Turkey. Emu's legs grew stronger, and soon he was able to run as fast as the other could fly. The strangest thing of all was that Dinewan seemed to become more and more friendly with him as the days and months passed by. At first Goomblegubbon was suspicious; but at last he came to the conclusion that Emu was even more simple than he had thought.

It was summer again. Everywhere the young fledglings were twittering and crying for food. Their parents were kept busy from sun-up to sun-down supplying them with things to eat. One morning Dinewan took his two biggest children out with him, leaving the remaining fourteen in their mother's care. The eldest children ran after their father, their little legs twinkling as they tried to keep up with him. Goomblegubbon and his wife were foraging in the scrub, surrounded by a noisy brood of children.

'Busy?' asked Dinewan.

'Busy!' Goomblegubbon said. 'We have to work all day long to keep all their bellies full. We're trying to get them to hunt for their own food, but we haven't had much luck so far.'

'Yes, they're rather scrawny, aren't they? The trouble is that there are too many of them. They don't get a chance to grow big.'

'What do you mean? You have plenty of children of your own.'

'Not now,' Dinewan said airily. 'We have disposed of most of them.'

'But why?' cried Turkey's wife.

'Well, we came to the conclusion that the only way to have strong, healthy chicks was to keep the best of them and get rid of the others. Look at them,' he said proudly. 'See how much bigger they are than your brood. The Dinewans of the next generation will be real birds.'

'There is something in what you say,' Goomblegubbon said thoughtfully. 'What do you think?' he asked his wife.

She had been walking round the Emu chicks looking at them from every angle.

'Yes, Dinewan might be right. There's no doubt that the young Emus are a credit to their mother.'

'Think about it,' Emu said, and strode off with the two chicks running after him.

'We can't let Dinewan have the laugh on us,' Goomblegubbon said. 'Come, wife. We will pick out our two biggest and kill all the rest. If we feed them to the eldest children they may grow even stronger than the Emu chicks.'

He met Emu on the plain the following day.

'I have taken your advice,' he said. 'Here are my two biggest Goomblegubbons. The others have gone. What do you think of these bonny birds?'

Dinewan began to laugh, and a shaft of fear shot through Goomblegubbon's heart.

'What are you laughing at, Dinewan?'

Emu called to his wife and she came out of the scrub leading a brood of sixteen young chickens.

'What a simpleton you are, Goomblegubbon,' he said, using the words that he had remembered for a whole year. 'A bird's strength lies not in his ability to use his wings, but in the number of his offspring. I am sorry for you, my friend, but perhaps it will teach you that Bustards are even more foolish than Emus.'

That is why Emus have many children but cannot fly, and why Bustards lay only two eggs each year.

 The Dance of Brolga

Brolga was the best dancer in her tribe, but to say this is to do her less than justice. She seemed not to be made of flesh and blood, but of the very spirit of the dance. Her back was straight, but it could bend like a tree in the wind, and her feet were as dainty and full of life as butterflies. Her hands were like little leaves that flutter in the breeze; and when she danced round the camp fires men thought that the Spirit of Earth had returned to them. There was a song in her every movement, and with her steps she charmed the hearts of men and women. There were no dull tasks for Brolga. To see her was enough, and other women were glad to take their yam-sticks and dig for roots to provide her with food.

Brolga ate very little. Her whole life was given over to dancing. It seemed that honey, and water, and the cool night air were all she needed to keep her restless spirit in her body. There was dignity and grace in every movement. The gay dancing of leaves on trees, the swift movement of insects, the sinuous slithering of the snake, the bubbling joy of running water, the slow, majestic rising of sun and moon, the soft shining of stars: all these could be seen as she danced.

Even the winds caressed her, and the Wurrawilberoos longed to possess her for themselves. The Wurrawilberoos were the boisterous whirlwinds that raised dust devils on the plains and pestered the camps of men and women. They were greatly feared, and were only kept at bay by the sharp spear points of the hunters and their frenzied shouting when the dust devils invaded their gunyahs and camp fires.

Brolga sought no man and feared no whirlwind. She was equally at home on the dusty plain and in the flickering light of the camp fires, and her dancing feet led her wherever she fancied.

Her mother went fossicking with her yam-stick one day, and Brolga danced along with her, weaving round the older woman a web of intricate pattern that failed even to disturb the dust. Far away rose the gaunt bones of a mountain range, where two exuberant Wurrawilberoos lived amongst the valleys. They saw the shimmering pattern that Brolga was weaving, far away from the protection of the warriors of her tribe. Shouting to each other in glee, they raced down the mountain slopes and out across the plain.

The two women were smothered in spinning dust and before they had realised what was happening, the Wurrawilberoos had snatched them up and carried them off to their hiding places. As they whirled round they laughed to think how easy it had been to capture such a rich prize.

'This creature of air and movement I will keep to dance for me,' one of them said. 'The old woman is well-nourished and tender. She will make a good meal as we sit by the fire looking at Brolga dancing for us tonight.'

'That's all very well,' grumbled the other Wurrawilberoo. 'She is as light as a feather, but this old woman is heavy, and I have her stone axe to carry as well.'

'Give it to me. I'll make Brolga carry it.'

He took the sharp axe and tucked it into Brolga's waistband, but when his attention was distracted she dropped it on the ground.

Burdened as they were, it took the Wurrawilberoos a long time to reach their home.

'Hurry up. I'm hungry. Where is the axe?'

The other Whirlwind, whose fingers were busy caressing the young woman, felt for the axe in her girdle.

'Its gone!' he exclaimed. 'Girl, where have you put it?'

Brolga laughed.

'You will not find it in a hurry. I dropped it on the sand many miles away.'

The Wurrawilberoos glared at each other.

'Go and fetch it,' said the one who had carried the old lady. 'It's your fault that it is lost.'

'And leave you with Brolga? That's the last thing I would do! You might run off with her.'

'If you won't trust me, I won't trust you. We had better go together.'

As soon as the whirling Wurrawilberoos had roared off down the valley, Brolga caught her mother's hand and together they climbed to the crest of the mountain, descended another valley, and raced across the plain, where they could see their own camp fires twinkling in the gathering darkness. The young woman tugged at her mother's hand and kept looking over her shoulder. Before long she saw two swirling clouds of dust and knew that the Wurra-wilberoos were after them.

'Faster, faster,' she urged.

The old woman was too exhausted to hurry. She sank to her knees and begged her daughter to go on without her.

Brolga did not waste breath in words. Summoning all her strength, she lifted her mother up in her slender arms and staggered on. Her feet were no longer light as a breath of air upon the sand. They sank deep, and her progress was painfully slow. She called out, and the hunters heard her. As they sprang to their feet they saw the furious whirlwinds about to leap on the two women. They ran out into the dusk, shouting at the top of their voices, and stabbing at the wind with their spears.

They were in time to save Brolga's mother; but the girl stumbled and was swept from their sight in the swirling dust.

The triumphant Wurrawilberoo retreated with his prey; and that was the last that was seen of Brolga until one day, long afterwards, a tall and stately bird walked up to the encampment.

To the amazement of the watchers in the camp it began a dance so beautiful that it reminded them of the dearly-loved girl they had lost.

'It must be Brolga!' someone cried. There was no doubt about it. Here were the same grace and poetry of motion, the same rhythm, the same aban-donment to utter ecstasy of movement.

'Where have you been?' they cried, but she could not reply. She pointed with her beak towards the sky, and they realised that the Wurrawilberoo had made his home somewhere in the blue heavens, leaving the dancing girl behind in the form of Brolga, the Native Companion.

Perhaps it is an injustice to accuse the Wurrawilberoos of capturing the women, for there is another tribal tale which says that they were taken away by two cannibals. They made their escape and returned to their own people, but the cannibals came back at nightfall and stole them away a second time. When the tribespeople discovered their loss they called on Wurrawilberoo, the beneficent Spirit of the Whirlwind, to help them.

The Spirit rapidly overtook the cannibals and whirled round them until they were forced to cling to trees to keep their feet. They dropped their burdens, but the one who was carrying Brolga muttered a spell.

The thud of racing feet was heard and they saw the hunters running swiftly with their spears levelled at them. Wurrawilberoo was not to be denied his prey. He increased his efforts, the trees were lifted out of the ground with the cannibals still clinging to them, and hurled into space. Neither the trees nor the cannibals were ever seen again.

The old woman lay in a heap on the ground. They lifted her up and carried her back to camp, but they could see no trace of their dearly-loved young woman. The spell that had been cast on her had turned her into a graceful bird which tried, but failed, to speak. Then it danced majestically before them, and they knew that in Native Companion they would always have a dancing girl to watch and admire.

 ## Why Mallee Bird Lays Her Eggs in the Sand

Wayambeh, a descendant of the original Wayambeh, who was turned into a tortoise, married Kookaburra. It was a strange mating, with an even stranger consequence.

Tortoises lay their eggs in the sand close to streams and billabongs, leaving them to hatch out for themselves, whereas kookaburras are like all sensible birds: they build nests and keep the eggs warm with their own bodies.

Kookaburra argued with his tortoise wife.

'It's not right,' he protested. 'Whoever heard of anyone burying eggs in the sand, just as if they were rubbish to be disposed of? Don't be so silly, Wayambeh. Do the sensible thing. I'll help you build a nest and then you can do your duty as a mother in the proper way.'

Tortoise darted her head from side to side in exasperation.

'I don't know why I ever married you, you silly bird. A fine figure I would make climbing a tree!'

'If my mother could lay her eggs in a nest, surely it's good enough for you?'

Wayambeh danced with rage, her shell jumping up and down on her back.

'Can't you get it into your thick head that I can't fly, I can't climb trees, I can't build nests, and if I sat on my eggs I would break them?'

She waddled down to the stream. Kookaburra flew overhead keeping a sharp eye on her; but once she settled down she remained motionless for so long that he grew tired of watching and flew off to get some food.

Presently Ouyouboolooey the Black Snake came by. He was an old friend of Wayambeh. She was glad to confide in him. Ouyouboolooey was a sympathetic listener. And it was at this moment that Kookaburra returned.

He gave a cry of rage, swooped down, caught Black Snake by the neck, flew to the top of a tree with him, and dropped him on the ground. Ouyouboolooey's back was broken. While he lay writhing in his death struggles, Kookaburra opened his beak and gave a great laugh: *Goor-gour-gah-gah!* and from the exultant, chattering laugh he gained his true name, Goorgourgahgah.

Although his wife was innocent of any liason with Ouyouboolooey, she was terrified of her husband's anger. She scuttled off swiftly on her short legs, but her time of egg-laying had come and could not be delayed. The instincts of a long line of ancestors were not to be denied, no matter what her husband might think. So she scooped a hole in the mud with her hind legs and laid six white eggs in it, covered them over, and smoothed the mud with her lower shell.

She had an interested spectator—Woggoon, the Mallee Fowl.

'Why do you lay your eggs there?' she asked. 'It seems a silly thing to do.'

'Nothing of the sort,' retorted Wayambeh. 'It's much more sensible than laying them in a nest high up in a tree, or even in the grass, and sitting on them to keep them warm.'

'If we didn't keep them warm the chicks would die of cold.'

'Ah, that is true. They must be kept warm. You see, that is why I lay mine in the mud. They are close to the surface where they are kept warm by the sun. We don't have to hatch them out, so you can see how much trouble we are saved.'

'I see,' said Woggoon thoughtfully.

She flew away and spoke seriously to her husband.

'I'm not going to lay my eggs in the nest this year,' she told him.

He laughed.

'Then where do you propose to lay them, my dear? Perhaps you thought of burying them somewhere!'

'That's just what I am going to do,' she retorted.

The argument between husband and wife raged all night long, but by morning the male bird was worn out and gave in. He even took part in the experiment, helping her to make a mound of leaves, sticks, and sand, and scraping a hole in which to bury her eggs.

Once the eggs were laid they were covered over. The two birds were not completely satisfied that Wayambeh's method would be successful. Day after day they visited the nest but saw no signs of the fledglings emerging. At last the female could stand the suspense no longer.

'My chicks are dead!' she wailed. 'They should have hatched out long ago.'

She scratched the soil from the mound. To her dismay she found only a few broken shells where her lovely eggs had been. But at that moment she looked up and saw the gladdest sight of her life. Coming towards her were several adorable little Mallee Fowl chickens whom she recognised at once as her own. The great experiment had proved successful. Ever since then Woggoon has followed Wayambeh's example and has laid her eggs in leaf-mould so they will hatch in the warm earth.

Part II

Legends of River, Lake and Shore

 The Frog Who Caused a Flood

In Central Australia and the western districts of New South Wales there are frogs which survive droughts by distending themselves with water until they are as round as balls. Then they bury themselves and wait for the rains to come again. In dry weather the aborigines dig up the frogs and drink the water with which their bodies are filled.

These little frogs may well be descended from Tiddalick, an enormous frog which lived in the far off days when men first came to Australia. Who can tell how big he was? Did he tower over the hills, and did the earth shake when he moved his feet?

There came a day when Tiddalick was thirsty. He drank the water of the nearest river until it was quite dry, and nothing was left but black mud at the bottom of a long trench. He roamed further afield in search of water, for his thirst was not yet quenched. Wherever he went billabongs, lakes, and streams disappeared into his vast mouth, until there was no more water left in all the land.

Animals and men gathered together in great distress. Every drop of water was contained in Tiddalick's swollen stomach. By this time he had drunk so much that he was unable to move.

There was still no sign of rain. The only way that water could possibly be obtained was to get it back from Tiddalick. Spears and boomerangs were useless, because the monster frog would not feel them however hard they were hurled at him.

'We must make him laugh,' said Goorgourgahgah the Kookaburra. 'If only we can do that, then he will have to hold his hands against his sides and the water will pour out of his mouth.'

'Very good,' said Kangaroo. 'You try and make him laugh. You're the best laugher in the bush.'

Goorgourgahgah perched on a branch close to Tiddalick's head, and his chattering laugh rang out again and again.

'Goorgourgahgah, Goorgourgahgah,' it went, and his beak clattered incessantly. 'Come on, Tiddalick, laugh, you big, fat, bloated, squelchy frog. If you could see yourself squatting there like a bursting pot, you'd laugh till you cried. Goorgourgahgah, Goorgourgahgah!'

Tiddalick moved his head very deliberately and looked at Kookaburra with round, wet, mournful eyes. There was not even the shadow of a smile on his wide and doleful face.

'I give up. I can't laugh any more,' Kookaburra cried. 'Who will try next?'

They all tried. Some of them danced and turned somersaults, and the men told funny stories, but their exertions made them even more thirsty, and Tiddalick seemed to have gone to sleep.

The last to try was Noyang the Eel. He was their final hope. He turned himself into a hoop, he wriggled and rolled over and over on the sand, and even stood upright on his tail, spinning round like Wurrawilberoo the whirlwind.

A tiny smile began to creep slowly over Tiddalick's face and a river of water splashed out of the corner of his mouth. Men and animals rushed forward and drank before it disappeared into the dry sand. Noyang went on spinning on the point of his tail, faster and faster, till he could scarcely be seen.

Tiddalick started to chuckle. The grin spread further across his face, and more water slopped out. Deep rumbles came up from his belly, and soon he was laughing so helplessly that he put his hands to his sides and rocked to and fro. His mouth opened wide and a great smooth tide of water came gushing out. It swept the men and animals away, and soon Tiddalick was a poor, shrunken little frog, while as far as could be seen a shining lake of water spread over the land.

Why Frogs Croak and Lyre Birds Sing

The name by which the green frog was known to animals was 'Son of the Clear-running Stream'. This is the legend which tells why such a beautiful name was given to him by the Lyre Bird.

There was a little stream on the western slope of the Blue Mountains which feeds the Murray River. It was cooled by overhanging trees, warmed by sparkling sunlight, and tickled into ripples by the friendly breeze. It sang an unending song of joy, and whenever it raced over pebbles in its bed or tumbled from one step of the mountain to another, thousands of little bubbles came popping to the surface. All playful little streams are full of bubbles, but only in this one tiny river was each bubble alive. They were the crystal homes of tiny water spirits which looked out from their clear cages and danced in tune with the song of the stream.

Only one river with water spirits living in the bubbles; only one bubble with a water spirit which longed so much to play with the floating twigs and the dancing sunbeams that it wished and wished until at last it turned into a living creature: a tiny little green frog. But he could not escape from his crystal prison. It bobbed up and down in the water, swirled round in the eddies, and sometimes sprang right out of the water in its struggles, falling back with a musical splash, sinking to the bottom, and bursting up into the sunshine again.

When evening came the stately Lyre Bird stepped down to the stream to drink. He was used to seeing the dancing bubbles, but on this special evening of spring he noticed that one of them seemed different to the others. It was bouncing higher, and was not as clear as air. Inside it, something green glinted in the twilight. Lyre Bird released a trill of sound like the tiny notes of a Bellbird. The bubble danced even more excitedly. Watching it closely, Lyre Bird sang the songs of many birds, mingled with the happy notes of running water.

After a while he grew tired of seeing the bubble dancing and prepared to go home, but a spirit voice sounded in his ear. It was the Great Spirit himself who had taken pity on his tiny water spirit.

'Keep on singing, Lyre Bird,' said the Great Spirit. 'It is one of my little ones you are seeing in that bubble. Your song is bringing it to life, and soon the bubble will shatter and it will be released and become a living creature of the stream.'

Filled with importance, and with a feeling of tenderness, Lyre Bird sang until he felt his throat would burst. And at last, as the sun rested on the hills, the bubble was gone and a tiny creature with a green body and arms and legs swam up through the water and sprang on to a broad leaf. Its sides palpitated, and its mouth opened and shut, but no sound came out of its open mouth.

'Go on, sing!' Lyre Bird said; but the little frog could make no sound.

'Teach him to sing,' said the Great Spirit, and Lyre Bird stood on the bank singing on and on into the night, until at last the little frog opened his mouth very wide and gave one tiny croak.

'That's enough for tonight,' Lyre Bird said to him. 'Stay there and I will come back tomorrow and give you another lesson.'

In the morning the frog was waiting there on the leaf when Lyre Bird came down to the stream.

'Good morning, Son of the Clear-running Stream,' he said to the frog. 'I want you to listen carefully today, and do your best to copy me.'

By the end of the day the frog could sing a few notes. Day after day Lyre Bird went back, and at last became proud of his tiny pupil. The time came when the Son of the Clear-running Stream surprised him. He had come down to his favourite place on the bank and was looking about for the frog, when he heard his brother's voice in the bushes behind him. He swung round, but no one was there. He turned back and saw the frog holding his sides and trying not to laugh.

'You wicked little fellow,' he chided him. 'So you've learned to throw your voice too. The time has come for the others to hear you.'

He sent out messengers calling all the birds and animals to come to the stream to listen to the water spirit singing his song. It was a selfless act. Lyre Bird was more proud of his pupil than he was of his own singing.

It was a wonderful occasion. By nightfall all the birds and animals had assembled and a silvery moon made a fairyland of the stream and the glade through which it flowed.

'Wake up,' called Lyre Bird. He knew that when the little green frog was asleep, it was at home with the other water spirits. Presently a small head and two bulging eyes appeared above the water.

'Here he is,' Lyre Bird said, and they all began to laugh at the funny little creature which hopped on to a leaf and puffed out his tiny chest.

'What is it?' they asked Lyre Bird. 'Have you brought us here just to see this absurd little object that looks like a bloated man?'

'Not to see him,' Lyre Bird said, 'to hear him.'

All through that night, as the moon sailed majestically across the sky, they sat and listened to the singing of the frog who was called Son of the Clear-running Stream. In the enchantment of his voice they heard the sound of running water and tumbling waterfalls, of soft wind in the trees and raindrops thudding on the ground, the songs of the birds and the cries of animals and insects. All these sounds came from the swelling throat of the little green frog.

When it was over Lyre Bird said, 'I am proud of you. You can sing better than I.'

Green frog dived into the water to hide the fierce pride that shone in his eyes. 'I am the best singer in the whole world!' he said to himself. 'I am better than Lyre Bird!'

But it was lonely in the stream all by himself. The Great Spirit took pity on him a second time, and sent another frog to him as a wife.

'I am the best singer in the world,' he said to his wife. 'I could charm the moon down from the sky—if I wanted to.'

'Let's see you do it,' said his wife.

Son of the Clear-running Stream sat on the broad leaf close to the bank and sang and sang till he was on the point of bursting. The moon sailed serenely on and took no notice. Green Frog sang louder still and then, suddenly, his voice broke and all that came out was a harsh croak.

The sons of the clear-running stream can still throw their voices; but who wants to hear them when all they can do is croak harshly? It is the Lyre Bird, the patient teacher of the green frog, to whom men listen.

 ## The Miracle of Spring

It was when young Cockatoo, so full of life, splendid in white feathers and proud yellow crest, fell from the nest and lay lifeless on the ground, that living things realised for the first time that there was a mystery they could not solve.

They circled the pathetic bunch of feathers, speaking to it, trying to bring back the spark of life. A few days later, when his body had begun to disintegrate and return to the earth from which it was made, a meeting was held. Everyone was there except Narahdarn the Bat, of whom strange rumours had begun to circulate. They turned first to Wungghee the Mopoke, who sat so still and looked so wise; but Wungghee had no answer to the question, 'What has happened to Ouyarh?' He turned his head slowly from side to side and looked at them with round, staring eyes, but had nothing to say.

Then Mullian spread and fanned his wings, and the waiting circle of creatures looked at him expectantly.

'Wungghee has no words that will fit this new thing,' Mullian said, 'but I, who am at home in the sky, can tell you what happened to Ouyarh.'

He picked up a stone in his beak and dropped it in the river. There was a tiny splash, a spreading of ripples, and the stone was gone. Mullian said no more, but by his action they knew that he meant that Ouyarh had gone into another world, perhaps into another life, and that when his body wasted away they would not see him again.

The ripples had hardly died away when Wahn shook his head and squawked angrily.

'Mullian knows only a part of the mystery,' he said. He picked up a piece of wood, flew over the river, and dropped it into the water.

'Watch,' he said as the chip fell from his beak.

They lined the river bank. The chip sank beneath the water, but soon it emerged a little lower down the stream, bobbing in the current.

'What does that mean?' asked a Bandicoot.

'The chip is Ouyarh,' Wahn explained. 'Do you all understand that?'

'Yes,' they chorused.

'Ouyarh is dead. He has left us, and all we now see is his body. That is not the real Ouyarh. It is only skin and feathers, muscles and liver and entrails. The real Ouyarh stays alive. He leaves his body behind and goes into that other world that Mullian has told you about. But his spirit lives. It lives! Perhaps it stays in the other world sometimes, like Mullian's stone, but I say that it is like my piece of wood, and that it floats back to life.'

There was a tumult of noise and chatter as animals and insects discussed the matter. It was another Cockatoo who called for silence.

'These may be wise words,' he said, when at last he could make himself heard, 'but who can tell whether Mullian is right or whether Wahn has the words of wisdom? Sticks and stones are all very well, but no one knows where the truth lies until it is proved by some living thing that Baiame has made.'

Silence fell at once, for it was obvious that what Cockatoo had said was right.

Warreen the Wombat was the first to volunteer.

'I will go to the other land,' he said. Then he gurgled deep in his throat and they knew that he was laughing. 'It's one way to prove something. If I don't come back you will know that Mullian is right, but the only one who will know what has happened will be me.'

'We'll go too,' said Beewee the Goanna, Bilbie the Bandicoot, and Ouy-ouboolooey the Black Snake.

'Very good,' said Cockatoo. 'When will you come back to us? That is, if you do come back,' he added.

The volunteers conferred together.

'We shall return in the springtime, when Yarrageh fastens the flowers on the trees and carpets the grass with colour. We shall return if it is the will of Baiame that we should do so.'

The meeting dispersed, and Wombat, Goanna, Bandicoot, and Black Snake disappeared into holes in the ground and hollow trees, curled up tightly, and went to sleep.

The winter months passed slowly by. Sometimes the birds and animals and insects thought of their friends who had gone into the long sleep, and wondered if their spirits would come back to earth renewed and youthful again.

But when Yarrageh spread glowing colours over mountain and plain with a lavish hand, and the daring animals returned, everyone was disappointed. They were the same old Wombat, Goanna, Bandicoot, and Snake, thinner and bedraggled. All the winter they had been living on their own fat. There was no new life, no spirit that Wahn had told them would rise from their dead bodies.

'My words have not been proved,' Wahn admitted, 'but neither have they been proved wrong. Nor do we know whether Mullian was right or not.'

'Look at me,' said Ouyoubooloooey. 'At least I have a new skin.'

He wound sinuously among the animals, showing off his bright new scales.

'What shall we do now?' someone asked sadly.

There came a shrill piping from the insects.

'We want to help!' they cried.

The birds and animals laughed. Kookaburra's laugh went on so long that it seemed as though it would never stop. The insects were angry.

'You despise us because we are tiny; but you will never understand the mystery unless we help you.'

'Very well,' said Kookaburra, feeling sorry he had hurt the feelings of the little people. 'I'm sorry I laughed.'

He turned and spoke to the others. 'The animals and reptiles failed,' he reminded them. 'It can do no harm to let the little ones try.'

island, because that was all that was left of it, and as far
re was water everywhere.'

f help!' Dinewan sneered. 'I dreamed I was on a flat plain
he birds and animals and snakes were fighting each other.
ong that none of them were left alive, and the plain was
es. And that's just what will happen unless we do some-
e added savagely. 'Perhaps Kangaroo had a wonderful
ll us what to do about it?'

dream, Dinewan. All night I lay awake. I kept thinking
und yesterday. It may well be that Baiame has put this
a purpose. Let us go and look at it.'

ollowed Kangaroo to the place where the bone was lying
u dug with his strong claws and uncovered other bones.
ting in the same direction.

on for this,' Deereeree twittered.

at it is,' croaked Dinewan.

up the bone he had first discovered.

in it,' he shouted excitedly. 'I can feel it inside me.'

of the bone into the ground and pushed against it. It
ccord, with Mirram holding on to one end and the birds
followed the direction in which the other bones were
deep trench behind it. There was a sudden roar, and
ked back they saw white-capped waves and a torrent
vn the channel that the bone had made.

wave I saw in my dream,' cried Deereeree.

ran faster, and the water raced behind them, filling the
he marsh lands, flooding the lagoons until they over-
trees and rushes were submerged. The lizards and
nd as fast as their legs would carry them. The birds
d and flew from their homes. By nightfall not a single
be seen. The fertile marshes lay underneath a single
ing right out to the horizon.

They agreed. When autumn came the grubs and insects burrowed into the soil, crawled up the tree trunks, and hid in crevices in the bark, or swam under water and clung to the stalks of water-plants.

But no one had really taken them seriously. It was a long cold winter. Some of the birds had flown away to warmer lands, and anyone who remained was so busy keeping warm and seeking food that he forgot all about the bravery of the insect people. Snake, Wombat, Goanna, and Bandicoot were fast asleep, for they had found that it was an easy way to survive the rigours of the winter season.

Yarrageh had scarcely begun another season's labour of love when the Swifts came flying down to earth, chirping, excitedly, and calling the animals and birds together.

'We have seen something new, something new,' they sang. 'We have followed the path of Yarrageh, and now he has come to you, to you, to you.'

The animals gathered together expectantly. Presently they saw little moving specks of colour on the ground. They were the tribe of Beetles, resplendent in flashing metallic armour. Then a sharp-eyed bird saw a grey chrysalis hanging from a tree. The chrysalis opened, a butterfly emerged, and spread its delicate wings, fanning them slowly to and fro as if to dry them in the warm breeze. Something climbed out of the river and hung from a swaying stem. Wings, almost transparent, gradually unfolded and a long shining body stiffened and came to life in the sunshine. With a whirr of wings it flew up, hovering like a rainbow above them.

Butterflies and moths and insects of every shape and size, resplendent in their new dress, fluttered and swooped and ran among the birds and animals.

'So it is true,' Wahn shouted triumphantly. 'These are new insects. They have been born again with new spirits and new bodies. There *is* another world, and they have come to tell us that death is not the end of life.'

This was the miracle of spring; the miracle that returns every year when Yarrageh comes with warm, gentle breezes and fingers gay with colour.

The Digging Bone

In the Northern Territory, where a gulf bites deeply into the land, lagoons and marshes once extended far inland. They teemed with wildfowl, and on the drier parts animals were to be found everywhere. The birds and the animals lived happily together; there was plenty of food, and they were content to share the beautiful earth and water. But with the passing years the birds became jealous of the animals and lizards who came to the edge of the lagoons to drink, and who dared to swim in the water the birds regarded as their own.

'From now on you must keep to your own place,' said the birds. 'There is plenty of room for you on the land. If you are thirsty you can drink from the streams and the small pools, but you must leave the marshes to us. They are our homes. We build our nests there. You trample our grass, and you crush our reeds, and you dirty our water. Keep to your own place.'

The animals and lizards resented being ordered away from the lagoons which they regarded as their home just as much as the dry land.

'There is plenty of room for everyone in the marshes,' they complained, 'and there is very little dry land. It will be overcrowded if we have to stay there. We'll begin to fight among ourselves if we are not allowed to roam where we want. We have just as much right to the marshes and the lagoons as you.'

'Keep out! Keep out!' screamed the birds. 'They are ours, not yours. Keep out!'

Then the animals and lizards banded together. They advanced on the lagoons like an army, swarming on the edges, breaking down the reeds, treading unwittingly on the nests of the wildfowl. The birds rose up in clouds and attacked them with beak and claw. The air was thick with flying feathers, and fur, skin, scales, and blood floated across the marsh water.

The battle seemed to go on endlessly. Hundreds of birds and creatures of the land rose to take the place of those who were killed. From every part of the marshes hoarse shouts, high-pitched screaming, angry roaring, and

the clash of weapons indicate
the living creatures were dea

The only ones who took
and Willy Wagtail. They me
the contestants, but they cou
screams.

'We must do something
garoo. 'It is sheer selfishne

'I am a bird, but I am a
Wagtail sadly. 'Selfishness
it out.'

'Fighting won't do it.'

'Ah, but there is one t
lands away from the bird

'But what would hap

'They would find and

'How could we poss
are only three of us. Eve
we would only cause m

'There is one way w
let the sea into the lag
would bring them to th

Dinewan the Emu
have to do,' he remar
with your little claws,

The bird hung its

'If we quarrel am
build a shelter and
answer in our dream

In the morning t

'In my dream,'
tidal wave rolled i

highest part of th
as I could see th

'That's a lot o
and everywhere t
They fought so l
covered with bon
thing about it,' h
dream that will te

'No, I had no
about a bone I fo
thought in me for

The two birds f
on the ground. Em
They were all poin

'There is a reas

'Then tell us wh
Mirram picked

'There is magic

He dug one end
moved of its own a
running after him. I
pointing, leaving a
when the friends lo
of water rushing do

'This is the tidal

The three friends
trench, spilling into
flowed, and all the
animals fled to dry l
rose up in a vast clou
bird or animal was to
sheet of water, stretch

That is how the great gulf was formed, and that was how the birds were cured of their selfishness. Ever since they have been content to share land and water with animals and reptiles.

 The Relentless Pursuit

In New South Wales two mighty rivers flow together, and at their junction is a deep, clear water hole, which was once the home of the monster Gurangatch. Descended from a long line of ancestors, some of whom were lizards and some fish, Gurangatch was half-lizard, half-fish. He had grown to an enormous size, but the deep hole at the confluence of the rivers was large enough to accomodate him and give him freedom to move about. On account of his size he was never molested by fish nor birds, nor even by man until one day Mirragen the Cat came that way.

Mirragen the Cat-man was the most famous fisherman in all that part of Australia. With net and spear he could seek out the wiliest fish and entangle it in the meshes, or impale it on his many-pronged spear. He did not rely on skill alone, but had also a knowledge of spells which would lure the fish from their hiding places and draw them within reach of his spear. He was a traveller, too, always seeking fish experiences, and priding himself on the many different kinds of fish he had caught and eaten. Little fish he despised. Only the biggest were considered fair game by Mirragen, and if they were large enough to provide sport as well as food, he was well content.

For a long time now he had had to satisfy himself with smaller fish from the rivers and lakes which were his usual hunting grounds, and he had become discontented.

'Remain here,' he had said to his family. 'You are safe in this valley, and there are plenty of roots and small game in the hills to keep hunger at bay. I am going away for a time. When I return I will bring back the biggest fish you have ever seen.'

They tried to dissuade him, but he was adamant.

'Eels!' he exclaimed scornfully, when they pointed out that the river by their camp was full of fat eels. 'They are lazy and easy to catch, and there is not a single one as long as my arm. They are food for babies. I am off to find a fish that is worthy of a man's skill.'

When he came to the junction of the two rivers his eyes lit up and his stride lengthened.

'The very place I am looking for!' he exclaimed.

Placing his dilly bag and fishing gear on the ground, he crawled forward on hands and knees and put his head over the edge of a cliff where he could look straight down into the water hole. At first he could see nothing but green water, but as his eyes grew accustomed to the gloom at the foot of the cliff, his gaze went deeper and deeper into the water, as though he were actually swimming through it. Further down he went, and suddenly he found that he was looking into two enormous, unblinking eyes.

'Gurangatch!'

The name came naturally to him, for he had heard vague rumours of an enormous reptile or fish that lived at the bottom of a deep pool where two rivers flowed together.

He repeated the most powerful spells he had learned from the wirinuns, and slowly Gurangatch floated towards the surface, struggling in vain against the unseen power that was drawing him upwards. The sweat ran down Mirragen's face and dropped into the water, but in spite of the magic power that was being exerted, he was unable to hold the monster, which drifted down once more into the safety of the water hole.

'Tomorrow!' he thought; and he sharpened the prongs of his spear before lying down to sleep. 'Tomorrow he will not escape me, even if I have to dive into the pool to transfix him with my spear. This is indeed the prize that I promised to bring home to my tribe. If I succeed, I shall be remembered for ever as the killer of Gurangatch.'

The monster was really frightened. For many years he had lived in the pool, confident that no one could harm him because of his size, and he had not been prepared for Mirragen's magic. He knew that when the sun rose the Cat-man would be waiting for him, armed with more than magic. Sure enough, when the sun's first rays lit the top of the cliff, Mirragen's spear flashed down and rang against his scales, but they were hard enough to turn the prongs. He waited for the next move, knowing that Mirragen's net would be equally useless, but dreading some new device that he would be powerless to resist. Presently he began to feel sleepy. It did not seem to matter any longer what Mirragen did, and his mind began to drift away on a tide of unconsciousness. He was brought back to life with a shock when he felt himself begin to float upwards. There was a strange taste in his mouth, and he knew that the Cat-man had poisoned the water with a tincture of bark. It was not sufficient to kill him, but enough to sharpen his senses and make him aware of the danger that was threatening him.

'I must get away from the pool before he catches me in the clutch of his magic powers,' he thought.

With a flick of his powerful tail he turned round and began to burrow into the solid rock. Leaving the home of his ancestors behind him, he swam through the ground almost as easily as if it were water. Earth, rocks, and sand were ploughed up in an immense wave, and as he wriggled through the new element, the river turned in its course and filled the channel with a foaming torrent of water.

Mirragen was not aware that Gurangatch had left, for he was hunting for more poisonous bark. When he returned he rubbed his eyes. A third mighty river was now flowing through the land, dwindling to a thread of silver in the far distance. Picking up his net and spears, he ran along the bank. Tiny landslides kept slipping in the river and he had to watch his steps lest he should slide down with them and be carried away in the flood.

As the heat of the day was ebbing he reached the end of the stream. It had changed course several times when Gurangatch had met with a solid outcrop of rock, but at last it had come to an end, and plunged underground.

Mirragen debated whether he should follow it into the cave where it disappeared, but he knew that he was no match for a monster in the dark chasms of the earth. He climbed a small hill above the cave and dug down into the soil until he felt it give way beneath him. Tying several of his fish spears together, he probed the hole, hoping that the monster might be somewhere beneath. Failing in this, he dug another, and another, but succeeded only in piercing the rock with deep holes which remain to this day above the Whambeyan caves to witness to his attempts to reach Gurangatch.

But the monster had felt the spear slithering past his flanks, and realised that if he stayed there he must fall victim to the relentless fisherman. Once again he dug through the ground, and as he twisted and turned he came out into the valley where Mirragen had left his family. They saw him coming. First the mighty head broke the side of the valley, then the great body slithered down the side almost to their feet, and along the furrow the water raced in a torrent like a tidal wave confined to a narrow bed. The water foamed over the edges and splashed against the rocks, licking at the heels of the women and children as they raced for safety up the far side of the valley.

There they met a weary man who had been travelling along the crest of the ridges.

'Mirragen, husband,' cried his wives, 'stay with us! We are afraid. The monster is devastating the land and we have barely escaped with our lives. Even if you were to catch up with him you could not overcome such a monster. Be satisfied with the eels in our little stream and remain with us.'

'There will be no eels here now, nor any little stream,' laughed Mirragen. 'The stream is a great river now, but it will be a long time before fish come into these waters. If I do not catch Gurangatch now I will never rest content. This is my destiny.'

He ran on and on, and by nightfall he had caught up with the lizard-fish. Mirragen's body and limbs were torn by sharp rocks and he was faint through loss of blood. He plunged his spears into the monster's side, but again the spear points glanced off the scales, and Gurangatch's tail swung round and knocked him off his feet. In the gathering darkness they fought, until the rocks were worn smooth. Gurangatch slid off them and resumed his journey, but Mirragen was now too tired and bruised to follow.

Morning came and he took up the chase again.

'He is getting weary, but so am I,' he thought. 'If we fight again I may get the worst of it. The time has come to get help.'

He turned back and went to a camp where he knew he would find some of his tribe. They were sitting down to their evening meal when he arrived, and greeted him enthusiastically.

'Welcome, Mirragen,' they cried. 'Have you brought some new fish for us to eat?'

The Cat-man sank down with a groan.

'I am weary and hurt,' he said. 'For day after day I have been following Gurangatch, and I have nearly caught him.'

They opened their eyes wide.

'Gurangatch? No one could ever hope to catch Gurangatch!'

'Well, I have!' Mirragen snapped. 'I cast magic spells over him. I poisoned the water where he lived and drove him out. I have been chasing him through valleys and over hills, and under the earth. He is at the point of death, and all that remains is to put an end to his sufferings. I am a generous man, so I invite you to help me and share the honour that will come to me.'

'Not us!' they said promptly. 'You don't look very fit, Mirragen. It looks as though you have been in a fight and have had the worst of it. We would rather stay here and eat the delicious eels we caught this morning.'

Mirragen got up with an exclamation of disgust. 'I will find someone else to share the glory,' he said.

'You might try the Bird-men further down the valley,' one of his relatives suggested.

As he stumbled off into the night Mirragen thought that this might be a good idea, especially if some of them were diving birds, for he suspected that Gurangatch had taken refuge in a water hole, and he was too tired to begin the whole sequence over again.

The Shags and Divers and Ducks were ready to help him, and they travelled with him along the trail that was so clearly marked by the newly-formed rivers, until in the morning they came to a large pool where the river ended, disappearing into the ground where Gurangatch in his struggles had formed the underground mazes of the Jenolan caves.

One of the Ducks paddled across the hole, bobbed his tail in the air, and sank down into the water. They waited a long time for him to return, but when he appeared he swam quickly to the bank, waddled ashore and began to walk back towards his home.

'What have you seen?' shouted Mirragen.

Duck flicked his tail and said shortly, 'The hole is bottomless. There's nothing there.'

Shag was the next to try. He fluttered over the water, closed his wings, and plummeted down into the depths. He came up with a small fish in his beak, which he brought ashore and laid at Mirragen's feet.

'Is this Gurangatch?' he asked.

The Cat-man was so exasperated that he kicked it back into the pool, and Shag fled in case he should do him an injury.

Only Diver Bird was left.

'Please try,' Mirragen begged. 'The others were afraid, but I know you will help me.'

Diver flew high up into the air and fell towards the pool like a flash of lightning. The water closed over him. He was gone so long that Mirragen began to fear for the life of his friend, but at last he bobbed up and swam ashore.

'Gurangatch is there,' Diver said, 'but you will never catch him. All I could do was to bring you a little part of the monster that I could carry in my beak.'

He gave a piece of flesh to his friend. It was covered with large silver scales that twinkled in the sunlight.

The Cat-man put his arm round the bird. 'You are my friend,' he said. 'It is the end of the chase. Let Gurangatch lie there for ever. We have his flesh and we will eat it together to show him that we are the victors.'

The flesh was soon eaten, but the Whambeyan and Jenolan caves, and many rivers of New South Wales, remain to show how Mirragen the Cat-man chased Gurangatch the monster in the Dreamtime and ate a piece of him as a token of victory.

 ## Kubbitha and the Tuckonies

In the days when there was no Murray River, Mungoongarlie the giant Goanna and his tribe lived by the banks of the Riverina. It was a good place to live until the drought came; then the river would dry up until only a few mud holes were left in its bed. The fierce sun beat down on them and sucked up all the moisture, leaving ugly cracks in the dried mud, and all the life of the valley was in danger. The animals began to die of thirst, and soon pathetic bundles of feathers and dehydrated bodies were lying on the ground.

The only creatures who seemed able to survive the great thirst were the Goannas. They had a secret supply of water hidden among the rocks; each day they went there to slake their thirst, but they guarded the secret and would never share it with others, not even with their own wives.

Kubbitha, the little Black Duck, the youngest wife of Mungoongarlie, begged her Goanna husband to allow the wives to share the water supply of the Goannas.

'And not only for us,' she said. 'You must have plenty of water, and if you share it with others you will have friends for life.'

'I don't want friends,' Mungoongarlie said. 'I'm quite well able to look after myself.'

'Dont you want wives? Without them you would soon be in trouble, especially when you want your meal prepared.'

'Get out,' Giant Goanna said roughly. 'If I share the water with anyone who asks for it, the supply will dry up and then we'll all be dead. And dead Goannas don't need wives.'

Kubbitha was a woman with a strong mind. She went to the other wives and said, 'Mungoongarlie will never show us where the water is, but I think we might find it ourselves. When we go out to look for roots tomorrow, let us follow the tracks of the Goannas. They will lead us to the water hole in the rocks. It must be somewhere in the mountains, because that is the direction they always take.'

So in the morning the women took their digging-sticks and set out across the plain. They scattered in various directions, but when they were well away from the camp they turned towards the hills. They searched all day, but in vain. The Goanna tracks were lost among the rocks, and though they poked into crevices with their yam-sticks they could find no sign of water. At last they realised that it was time to go home. They hurried back over the plain, but when their husbands asked them for food they had to admit that they had not been able to find any roots.

Mungoongarlie looked closely at his wife. His gaze dropped down to her feet.

'That is not the dust of the plain on your feet,' he said. 'It comes from the mountains. What have you been doing?'

'Looking for yams. I thought there might be some there.'

'Then what about the other women? Where have they been?'

'How should I know? I am not their husband.'

It was soon apparent that the Black Ducks had all been up in the mountains looking for water. The Goannas were angry with them.

'Listen to me,' Mungoongarlie said. 'Tomorrow morning all of us Goannas are going out on a hunting expedition. We will leave you one skin full of water, and that must last you till we come back. When we return we expect a big meal of roots and grubs, to go with the flesh we bring. Let's have no nonsense about looking for water. It will take you all the time to get the food ready.'

They left early in the morning before sun-up, and the women gathered round Kubbitha.

'What shall we do?' they asked. 'If we do not obey our husbands they will kill us, or make us die of thirst.'

'We shall die of thirst anyway, unless they show us where the water is,' Kubbitha replied. 'You may gather food, but I shall go to the mountains again. This time I will not return without the water!'

Two of the wives came with her while the rest of them went out on their daily tasks. The three women toiled up the mountain side. The sun beat against the rocks. Where there were cracks they were filled with fine dust and over all the heat rose in shimmering waves.

'It's no good,' one of the Black Ducks said at last. 'Without water we shall die before sundown. We must go back to where there is some shade.'

'You go back. I shall stay here. I have vowed not to return until I find water.'

Her friends were glad to get off the mountain side and into the shelter of the trees, but Kubbitha kept on searching. When she realised that she would not find the water that day, she built a shelter wall of stones at the entrance to a shallow cave and lay down to rest.

Sleep would not come. Her tongue was swollen and her head was aching. She felt she might be delirious, especially when she felt a cool touch on her hand. She started up in the darkness and saw, outlined against the mouth of the cave, a tiny man.

'A Tuckonie!' she gasped.

'Yes,' he said, 'and you are Kubbitha.'

'How do you know my name?'

'I know more about you than you think. I know what you are here for, and I have come here to help you. Follow me.'

In the growing light of dawn she followed him further up the mountain, until they came to a plateau. The morning mists lay in the hollows, and there was a delicious coolness as though water was not far away.

The little man put his hands to his mouth and gave a cry.

'Cooee!' It floated across the plateau and echoed from the cliffs above.

Presently more tiny figures appeared through the mist, and Kubbitha soon found herself surrounded by Tuckonies. They were friendly little creatures. They talked together in squeaky voices. After some argument the leader came back to Kubbitha.

'We have decided what to do. Go down to the foot of the mountain, Kubbitha. You will find your two friends coming to look for you. Send them back to their camp with the word that all the Black Ducks are to come to the mountain as quickly as they can.'

'What shall I do then?'

'You must climb up to this plateau again. It will be hot and tiring, and you may think that you will die of thirst on the way, but we know you are brave. Believe us, we are your friends, and we are trying to help you.'

Kubbitha did as she had been told. At the foot of the mountains she met her friends, who gave a cry of relief at seeing her.

'We thought you might have been carried away by the evil spirits of the mountain,' they said. 'Have you found the water?'

'Listen to me,' Kubbitha said. 'I have not found the water, but a wonderful thing is happening. I cannot tell you what it is because I do not know myself, but I am sure everything is going to be all right. The Tuckonies are helping us!'

The Black Ducks looked at each other and did not know what to say.

'Don't stand there doing nothing,' Kubbitha urged. 'Go back to the camp as quickly as you can. You'll be quite safe. The Goannas won't be back until later in the day. Tell all the women what has happened, and say that the Tuckonies want them all to gather here. Go quickly.'

They ran back, and Kubbitha turned to the mountain again. It was only the great heart of Kubbitha the Black Duck that took her back to the plateau. She arrived almost fainting and fell against the rocks.

'Here,' said the leader of the Tuckonies. He put her yam-stick, which she had left behind earlier in the morning, into her hand.

'Drive it deep into the heart of the mountain,' he said; then he vanished, and all his people with him.

Kubbitha rubbed her eyes. Perhaps the sun had made her see things that were not there? Perhaps it was all a device of the Evil One to drive her mad? But the Tuckonie's words still rang through her head, so she lifted her digging stick and thrust it into the ground. To her surprise it went down through the solid rock and disappeared from sight.

'Run, Kubbitha, run,' a voice drummed in her ears.

She turned and stumbled down the steep mountain side. Behind her there was hissing, rumbling sound as though all the mountain devils were at her heels. She dared not turn round to see what it was that was following her. The sounds became louder and she ran faster still. Everything was blurred in front of her and she could hardly recognise the Black Ducks until she fell into waiting arms, and heard a cry of rejoicing from them.

'Look, Kubbitha! Look at the gift you have brought from the Tuckonies!'

As the breath came back into her lungs she lifted her head, and saw a mountain stream tumbling down the mountains, piling itself up against the rocks, springing over them, dropping in smooth sheets, only to splash and rear up again, and finally to spread out across the plain at her feet in a shining band of silver. The thirsty sand tried to drink up the water, but the water flowed faster still from the unseen source above.

They turned to watch it as it swept on. Men and women and little children were running towards it, falling on their knees, and burying their heads in that blissful water. Birds and animals of all kinds mingled with them. All were drinking from the never-ending waters of the newly-born Murrumbidgee River.

Their thirst quenched, the Black Ducks returned to their camp, to find that they were on the wrong side of the new river.

'What shall we do?' they asked Kubbitha.

She laughed at them.

'We shall stay here, right where we are. Do you want to return to your husbands after what they have done to you?'

'No!' said the women with one voice. 'Besides, it is much more pleasant here than on the other side. Here there are trees and green bushes, but over there it is hot and dusty.'

At the end of that afternoon the Goannas returned to camp. They stared at the river in amazement, and then looked across to the other side. Mungoongarlie shouted to the wives. 'Come across and get our meal ready for us.'

The only reply was a chorus of mocking laughter.

'Never more,' Kubbitha called back. 'You would not be kind to us; now we shall never be kind to you.'

And since then Goannas have lived in hot and dusty places, while Black Ducks disport themselves in the cool waters of rivers and billabongs.

 The Monster of the Murray River

There were few terrifying monsters in Australia, but one could never be sure that an innocent lake might not conceal a dreadful Bunyip. And in some rivers there were fish or lizards like Gurangatch. Whowhie, the monster of the Murray River, was three or four times the length of the tallest man. He looked something like a Goanna, but was much more fearsome. He had a long tail, three legs on each side of his body, and the head of a frog. And he was an eater of flesh. No man or animal was safe when Whowhie was about, for he had an insatiable appetite.

The only thing that saved the tribes of the Murray River from extinction was that Whowhie was so large, his body so heavy, that he could move only slowly. As he dragged himself over the ground, the earth trembled; people knew that he was coming and were able to make their escape. He lived in a huge underground cave with many tunnels which led out to the bank of the river. When he came out of his lair, his feet stirred up the sand, forming the sandhills of the Riverina district.

It was at night that Whowhie was most feared. By day even the slowest animals could escape from him, but at night men and animals must sleep.

Whowhie learned the art of creeping silently through the darkness towards the gleam of a camp fire, picking up children, and older people too, without a sound and swallowing them whole. He was not satisfied with a small meal: twenty or thirty, or sixty persons at a time were not too many for Whowhie's capacious belly, and there was still room for unwary rats, wombats, wallabies, and even kangaroos as titbits for the feast.

The animal and human population of the district began to dwindle, and no one could go to sleep happily at night lest the monster should discover them in the darkness. To light a fire was dangerous, for it was a sign to him that food was waiting for him.

Sentries were posted, but Whowhie learned the art of appearing suddenly out of the darkness and engulfing them before they could shout a warning. In the finish the men and animals banded together to make plans to destroy the monster. Whowhie had raided one camp and had eaten everyone in the tribe—every single person with the exception of one small, terrified boy who had escaped to tell the news to others. It was decided that all the tribes should be assembled in an attempt to kill Whowhie, and that they should be summoned immediately. Whowhie could hardly move now on account of the enormous meal he had eaten, and it was felt that there was no reason for delay.

The water-rats who lived in little tunnels in the banks of the river reported that he had left a long trench behind him as he dragged his body back to his cave. There was no doubt that he had gone to the furthest part of the cave to sleep off the effects of his meal, and it would take him a week to get back to the entrance.

Fires were lit in several places and their smoke, rising in the still air, was the signal for the tribes to come together. Those who lived closest to the monster's cave were kept busy gathering shellfish and catching fish and cooking them to feed the visitors when they arrived. All day long the warriors trooped in to the river bank, carrying their sharpest and most deadly weapons, and eager to put an end to the terror of the Murray River. That night they held a feast, with much dancing and singing, for it had been a long time since they had dared to hold a corroboree, lest Whowhie should come on it unawares. This night all would be well, for he could not stir.

Early in the morning the water-rats explored the cave and reported that they could hear Whowhie puffing and snoring in the furthermost recess, and that it would be safe to enter. Piles of brushwood were dragged inside, and heaped up at the entrance to the cave. A torch was applied and the brushwood roared into flame. Green vegetation was piled on top of the fire and soon the cave was filled from end to end with dense, choking smoke. Above the crackling of twigs and the roaring of the flames the men could hear Whowhie coughing. The sound reverberated in the tunnels and grew louder as it reached the entrance, until it was like the roaring of wind in the pines or the crashing of waves on the seashore.

Day after day the fires burned on. The coughing and roaring grew louder as Whowhie staggered towards the open air. On the seventh day the warriors gathered in a half circle round the entrance, waiting expectantly.

A cloud of smoke billowed out of the tunnel, and through it lurched Whowhie, scattering the fire with his feet. His huge eyes were bloodshot, his skin blackened, his cavernous mouth opening and shutting as he gulped in the fresh air and expelled the smoke from his lungs. With one great shout the warriors fell upon him, thrusting their spears deep into his sides, beating him with clubs, and stripping the flesh from his body with their flint knives. Whowhie roared louder than ever, but his strength was ebbing fast. At length he tottered and fell, and the earth shook with the impact.

There has never been another Whowhie on the banks of the Murray River, for he lived alone without wife or family; but when the wind blows through the cave and echoes in the tunnels it is a reminder that the spirit of Whowhie lives on in the tortuous depths beneath the earth.

Part III

The Winjarning Brothers and Other Hero Stories

 ## How Wyju Made Red Ochre

As he drew near to the camp Wyju the traveller heard the lamentations of mourners.

'What is this?' he asked the first person he met. 'What is the matter?'

'One of our children has been swallowed by a huge snake that lives in the valley.'

Wyju was a kind-hearted man who spent much of his time helping others, and he was sad when he heard this.

'Have you killed it?' he asked.

'No. That is one of the reasons for our grief. You see, it was no ordinary Carpet Snake: there is a spirit in the snake, and we dare not touch it. If we did there would be no water left in our valley.'

'I know how it is,' Wyju agreed. 'But surely, if you were to kill it, and even if the streams flowed underground, you would be able to find them again?'

'It is easy to see that you are a stranger. If the great snake were to lie straight out with his head on the ground, we could kill him and there would be no trouble with the water; but, you see, he is always coiled up. We dare not touch him then because the water would go away and we would never find it again.'

'I think I know a way to make him stretch out his body,' Wyju said. 'Leave him to me.'

Followed by the curious glances of the tribesman, he searched till he found a mallee shrub. He dug its long root out of the ground and walked with it down the valley until he saw the carpet snake curled on a flat rock asleep in the sunshine. Taking care not to wake it, he climbed up into the branches of a tall tree which overhung the rock and lowered the mallee root until it dangled above the snake's head. Presently a few drops of water seeped out and fell on the snake; it stirred and opened its mouth so that the water fell on its tongue. Slowly it uncoiled its body and reached up towards the source of the water. When it was standing on the tip of its tail with its body as straight as a young tree, Wyju jumped off the branch and slid down the snake's body with his flint knife pressed into its belly. The snake shuddered and collapsed on the rock, and the missing child emerged unharmed from its limp body.

The tribesmen had been watching from a vantage point above the valley. When they saw that the snake was dead they swarmed down and bore Wyju back with them, giving him a tumultuous reception. The traveller was a quiet-spoken man, and his modesty only increased his popularity. News of his skill and daring spread to other tribes, and everyone spoke well of him. The uncles of eligible young women walked long distances to see him and offer their nieces in marriage. Wyju received them hospitably but excused himself.

'I am a restless man,' he told them. 'Though I am resting now with my friends, I am a solitary person, and no woman could keep up with me when the mood is on me. I would be a sore trial to any young woman.'

He did not tell them that his journeys gave him the opportunity of helping people in distress, for it was not his custom to speak of himself.

Through the encampment there passed an endless stream of men who were travelling towards Maljarna, where a rocky hill lifts out of a vast plain. Men who came to see Wyju and were unsuccessful in getting him to marry their nieces did not turn back but went on towards Maljarna.

'Seeing that I cannot agree to your proposals, why do you not return to your own tribe?' he asked one of the visiting men.

'I am looking for a husband for my niece.'

'I know; but I have already told you that I cannot accept her.'

'Ah, but there is always Kirkin. I must see him for myself. I would gladly give my niece in marriage to him, but ...'

He broke off and would say no more.

Slowly Wyju pieced together the story of Kirkin. He learned why men were so eager to visit him, and why they broke off their conversations so abruptly.

Kirkin, it seemed, was admired by men because of his hair, which was long and golden. Every morning he combed it out, and the rising sun seemed to turn it into living flame. He was always the centre of a large audience, not only of men, but of animals, birds, reptiles, and insects; all were fascinated by the sight.

The surprising thing was that they were all males. Women detested Kirkin because he was vain and boastful, and because they were jealous of his golden hair. If an uncle proposed that the man with the golden hair would make a good husband, the girls and women set up such an outcry that the man was glad to get away from them.

While Wyju was being sought vainly in marriage, Kirkin was thinking that, pleasant as it was to be admired by men, it would be much more satisfying if he had a wife to cook his meals and look after him. Even his closest friends had no hesitation in telling him about the women's dislike of him, nor in contrasting it with their eagerness to marry Wyju.

'Where does this wonderful man live?' he asked sarcastically.

When he was told that Wyju had no fixed abode, but at that time was not far away, he went to see the traveller.

'Why have you not come to pay your respects to me and see my golden hair?' he asked.

'I have been content to admire your reputation,' Wyju answered mildly. 'All men speak well of you.'

Kirkin saw that Wyju was a man not lightly to be taunted. He changed his tactics.

'And I have heard good things about you. We should be friends. Come to my camp and tomorrow I will show you how to catch a walliow,' he said.

'What is that?' asked Wyju.

'It has the finest flesh you ever tasted. It's something like a kangaroo-rat.'

Wyju accompanied Kirkin to his camp. As soon as he was asleep, his host went quietly into the long grass, and by the light of the moon he flattened it into the shape of a shallow coolamon, and buried long sticks in the ground. They had been sharpened, and hardened by fire. Kirkin set them with the points uppermost and tucked the flattened grass around them so they could not be seen. He put a dead animal on top and attached to it a cord which he led to a nearby bush.

In the morning Wyju gathered up his hunting weapons.

'You don't hunt walliow with weapons,' Kirkin laughed. 'We'll look for the nests together. When we find one you can kill it. All you have to do is to jump on the nest.'

They fossicked about in the long grass. Presently Kirkin whispered, 'Here, Wyju! Quietly! Lie down and peep through the grass. Tell me if you see anything move.'

'Yes, I see a nest,' Wyju exclaimed. He went down full length in the grass. While his attention was directed to the nest, Kirkin crept to the bush and pulled the string, causing the dead animal to move.

'He's there! He's there!' Wyju whispered.

'Jump on it now,' Kirkin said. 'Be sure you jump right in the middle of the nest.'

Wyju drew himself up to a sitting position with his legs under him. He sprang into the air and stamped both feet on the nest.

As the sharp spikes penetrated his feet he threw himself forward with a shriek of agony.

'Kirkin! Kirkin! Help! Something dreadful has happened.'

The man with the golden hair laughed aloud.

'You are an easy victim, my friend Wyju,' he gloated. 'That will teach you to come to me another time—if ever there is another time. See if the girls want to marry you now! I have plenty to do, so I am afraid I must leave you.'

He strode away laughing, while Wyju rolled in agony in the grass. He could not put his feet to the ground, nor could he bear to touch them to pull out the splinters. His blood kept on flowing until it filled the hollow where he was lying.

Long days and nights followed. The imprisoned Wyju kept struggling to free himself. Where his body threshed to and fro the earth became saturated with his blood and dyed a vivid red. In after years men made long journeys to that place to gather the red ochre that resulted from the mixing of Wyju's blood with the soil.

Sometimes he cried for help, and at last he was heard by the Great Spirit.

'It is the voice of Wyju who has helped so many of my children,' Baiame said to two famous hunters, the Winjarning brothers. 'Go quickly to his aid.'

Faster than the wind the brothers ran until they came to the bloodstained hollow where Wyju lay. Quickly and painlessly they removed the spikes that pierced his feet, and touched them with soothing fingers that relieved the pain. They lifted him to his feet and watched him as he took a few steps; then they disappeared.

'Tomorrow will be the last day this man with the golden hair will ever see,' Wyju muttered to himself. He waited till the first heralds of dawn sang their song, then he crept through the grass till he came to a place where he could see Kirkin clearly.

As the sun rose Kirkin glanced round to make sure that he could be seen by the men and animals who had gathered together to see his golden hair in the sunshine. Then he threw his hair up and forwards like a golden fan. At that moment Wyju stepped out of his hiding place and with one swift stroke of his boomerang severed Kirkin's neck. The head rolled down the rock and into the grass in a tangled net of golden hair.

Wyju picked up the body and put it on the fire, and that was the last of the man with the golden hair, except for a little bird that flew from his body looking for grubs and insects to keep alive.

Winjarning Brothers and the Evil One

Alone in an enchanted valley lived a man who was prematurely old. When he passed from boyhood to manhood and had completed his initiation tests, he had wandered off by himself and had discovered this lonely valley. It was known to the elders of the tribe, who feared it and never went near it. The rocks were twisted into fearsome shapes, and the valley was believed to be the abode of spirits. Knowing nothing of its reputation, the young man found it an idyllic place. A clear stream splashed and tumbled from pool to pool in a setting of grass terraces; trees and caves made cool shelters from the burning sun, and the valley teemed with life. Fish swam in every pool and animals provided an endless abundance of food.

'This is a good place for a man to live,' he thought.

Months passed like days and he could not bring himself to abandon a place which seemed so perfect. The only thing he needed was a wife to cook food and hold in his arms through the scented hours of the night. He remembered the young girl to whom he had been betrothed after the manhood rites.

'I will wait for her,' he reflected. 'She has been chosen for me. When the fullness of womanhood comes on her I will seek her out and bring her here to live with me.'

But when that time came the old desires had passed.

'I still want her, but it may well be that she has now seen other young men who are more attractive to her. I would not wish to spoil her life: I shall wait here and seek the will of the Great Spirit.'

Meanwhile the girl had grown up to desirable womanhood, and there were many young men who would gladly have taken her in marriage. Her tests had been conducted alone. From them she had emerged with even greater beauty. She had been told of the bridegroom who had been selected for her, and how he had disappeared into the enchanted valley where none dared follow him.

'He is old and we have no doubt he has become peculiar from living by himself for so long; but he is still your husband,' she was told.

The young woman was bewildered. At one time she thought of him as a man in the full strength of life, with whom she would find unimaginable delights; at other times she shuddered as she thought of him as a repulsive hermit who would feed on her beauty and drive her to work for him night and day.

'You have passed all the tests, Palpinkalare, but there is yet another ordeal. You are to go on a long journey, during which you will skirt the enchanted valley. This time you will not be alone. Your mother and I will go with you, but we shall not speak to you, nor you to us. And you will have eight companions to be your protectors. Four will be young men, and four will be elders who will give advice when you are in doubt.'

Her father turned away, and Palpinkalare's heart beat faster. Would she see her chosen husband? And if she did, what sort of man would he be?

The hunting party set off in high spirits. It was a further training period for Palpinkalare. During the day the young men taught her where to find edible plants and roots, how grubs and insects could be found by various signs, and how to follow the tracks of animals. At night the elders spoke to her, instructing her in the traditions and inner mysteries of her tribe. She had little time to think of the man who might soon be her husband, for sleep came quickly when she lay down late at night, and the young men roused her early in the morning.

One night she had a dream. She was overcome by a desire to find an enormous grub. In her dream she went to a tree and lifted a piece of bark. Underneath there was a round hole, almost large enough to accommodate her hand. She found a stick shaped like a hook and put it into the hole. Inside was something soft which moved when she prodded it. She drew it out and raised it to her mouth ... and then she woke.

In the morning she said, 'I must find a certain grub soon. A big one, larger than anyone has ever seen before. I dreamed about it last night, and now I am filled with longing for it.'

All day she kept referring to the wonderful grub of her dream. The elders looked at each other uneasily, and at night they sat apart from the others and conferred together.

'There is something wrong with Palpinkalare,' said one venerable old man. 'The dream and the craving for the grub are not natural. Something or someone has put the thought into her mind by taking possession of her spirit.'

'It must be Marmoo the Evil One,' said another, looking furtively over his shoulder into the darkness. 'We must sleep close together tonight and keep the fires replenished. Also we must take it in turn to watch.'

The others agreed, but the night hours passed uneventfully.

In the morning Palpinkalare rose before the others were awake and made her way to a certain tree which she recognised as the one she had seen in her dream. The bark hung loosely in exactly the same place. She lifted it and looked at the hole without surprise. There was the hooked stick, on the ground at the foot of the tree, waiting to be used. She caught the grub with the hook, pulled it out, raised it to her mouth, and turned round. And there, almost touching her, was the Evil One.

Half spirit, half man, and wholly evil, he had come across the track of eleven people some days before. After examining them, he came to the conclusion that there were five young people, one of them a girl; a man and his wife who walked apart from the others; and four old men. The Evil One had sat for a long time studying the tracks, and knew that the most important person was the young woman who was being guarded and educated by her companions.

He had followed the trail tirelessly for three days. When he came closer to the travellers he sent part of his mind ahead and probed the brain of the young woman. He discovered that, deep down, she was a prey to conflicting emotions, but that most of her thoughts were centred on her training. That night he had put the dream of the huge grub inside her subconscious mind; and now, on the fourth day, she was at his mercy.

Palpinkalare opened her mouth to scream, but no sound came. The Evil

One entered into her mind, which was filled with such a sense of horror that she fell down in a faint. The Evil One picked her up, threw her across his shoulders, and ran off with her. He climbed a hill and dropped down into a valley. It was the valley of enchantment where her betrothed husband lived. Reaching a grassy space, the Evil One laid the body of the young woman among the flowers and sat down to gloat over her beauty. His mind had lost contact with hers while she was unconscious.

Slowly Palpinkalare regained her senses. At first her mind was blank. Then she opened her eyes and saw blue sky above her, the graceful, drooping branches of the trees, and a riot of bright blossoms. She heard the song of a stream, smelled the perfume of the flowers: and then her eyes rested on the Evil One.

Now terrible sounds came from her throat. Scream after scream rang through the sunny valley, while the Evil One grinned as he listened. Slowly and deliberately he raised his spear and held it poised over the young woman.

The hermit of the valley was startled by the noise. It was the first time for years that he had heard the sound of a woman's voice. Picking up his waddy, he raced towards her. As he broke through the bushes a single glance showed the young woman sitting up, and the figure of the Evil One in the act of thrusting his spear into her body. Before he could move, or even shout, the spear point entered her heart. The Evil One looked up and saw a man bounding across the grass towards him. He shrunk back and vanished under the trees, while the hermit's waddy glanced harmlessly off the trunk of a tree.

The man stopped over Palpinkalare's lifeless body. In some mysterious way he knew that this was the girl who had been betrothed to him. She looked innocent and defenceless. Before he could even touch her living flesh, she had been snatched away from him. The tears rolled down his cheeks and beard and dropped on her face as he vowed he would dedicate his life to avenging her death.

There was consternation in the camp of the elders and the young men. They had called many times, but Palpinkalare had not answered. The young men had followed her footprints to a tree, where they found an enormous white grub lying on the ground. It took only a moment to find the footprints of a stranger, and to know that he had carried the girl away with him. The young warriors reported their discovery to the elders. The old one who had spoken the previous night was the first to speak again.

'I said the Evil One was not far away. We took what precautions we could, but he has outwitted us. We are no match for evil such as this. One of you young men must go to Palpinkalare's mother and father and tell them what has happened. The others must go to look for the Winjarning brothers. They are the only ones who can help us now.'

The others agreed. The young hunters ran quickly, and the following day they returned, bringing the famous wirinuns with them.

'Your daughter has been stolen by the Evil One,' the brothers told her parents. 'You must leave everything in our hands now. We shall take the young men with us; the rest of you will remain here until we come back.'

The Winjarning brothers were not frightened of the enchanted valley. When they saw that the trail led into it, they followed without hesitation, while the young men followed closely behind. They came to the sheltered glade, and their hearts sank. The body of Palpinkalare was wrapped in bark, and by its side knelt the hermit of the valley. There was no need for him to tell them what had happened. The events of the morning were written clearly on the earth and the grass, and their trained eyes could read every word of it.

'Help me to avenge her,' pleaded the lonely man, and the brothers agreed to do so.

'We cannot bring this lovely woman back to life,' they said. 'Her spirit has gone to the keeping of the Great Spirit, who must surely love her so much that he will not let her go. All we can do is to exact revenge, and to kill the Evil Spirit, body and soul, so that never again will he be able to harm mankind.'

The seven men followed the trail left by the Evil Spirit. It was not easy because he had run so swiftly and lightly that only the faintest impression of his feet remained, even on patches of sand. But the trackers were experienced men, and as darkness fell they saw the gleam of a distant camp fire.

'Let us go on through the darkness,' said the elder Winjarning. 'We can catch him unawares while he is sleeping.'

The words were scarcely out of his mouth when the fire began to spread, leaping from crest to crest of the hills, spreading like a living curtain along the mountain range. They knew now that their task would not be an easy one: the Evil One possessed powers that were denied to the wisest wirinuns.

They prepared their evening meal and waited for the morning. At first light they were on the trail again, and the sun had barely risen when they reached the deserted camping place.

'Look!' a young warrior exclaimed. 'He must have left as soon as we did this morning. He has passed us on the way.'

They retraced their footsteps hastily and reached the site of their own camp, which had been made on the edge of a steep valley. There was no sign of life except an emu which was cautiously picking its way down the slope. The Evil One's trail had stopped abruptly by a bare rock, and beyond it were the unmistakable prints of the emu's feet.

The younger Winjarning gave a shout.

'I have it!' he cried. 'The emu prints begin where the Evil One's left off. He has changed from a man to a bird.'

The hermit poked round among the bushes.

'Come here quickly,' he called to the others. They ran to him and he showed them the dead body of an emu. The legs and body were there, but the head and neck had gone, and no feathers were left on it.

'It is easy to see what has happened,' said the hermit. 'The Evil One has not changed into a bird. He has killed the emu and taken its feathers, its head and its neck, and covered himself with them. And he has made emu shoes for himself. We have not been looking at an emu at all, but at the Evil One himself, who has been walking with his back bent to make us think he was a bird. Let us go down into the valley and kill him.'

'No, not like that,' one of the Winjarnings warned him. 'Remember the camp fire that seemed to blaze for miles last night? He has many ways of deceiving us. We will spread out and approach the valley from different directions. When we are ready I will light a fire and send up a smoke signal. As soon as you see it, move in on him.'

They did as the Winjarning told them, and presently they were within a hundred yards of the emu. He was standing with his back to a rock ready to defend a narrow path which ended in a steep rock climb facing the open plain.

'We will never overcome him unless we use subtlety,' thought the elder Winjarning. He stepped behind a rock, where he was hidden from the Evil One, but whence he could see his younger brother. He made signs that the enemy should be attacked. Then, breaking off a long, straight branch from a tree, he tied a bundle of grass on the end, and held it up so that the Evil One could see it above the rock.

The sudden movement caught the Evil One's eye. He fitted a spear to his woomera, waiting to see what would happen. The grass tuft rose again, looking like a man's head. The Evil One stepped forward and threw his spear. At the same moment two spears flew towards him from the east and the north, entered his chest, and pierced his heart. The young Winjarning and the hermit had ended the Evil One's life.

Sad at the thought of the girl whose life had been taken, the men dragged the body of the Evil One down on to the plain, made a pyre of twigs and branches, and threw the body on top with its head to the north and its feet to the south as a sign of derision.

'Now begins the most important part of our task,' the elder Winjarning warned them. 'The body of the Evil One is dead but his spirit is still alive. It will try to escape, and it will take many forms. As soon as the fire is lit we must kill every living thing that crawls out of it.'

The flames roared up and consumed the ugly body. Without warning a full-grown kangaroo jumped out of the flames, and fell to the waddies of the young men. They threw it back into the fire; at once an eagle-hawk flew up with strongly-beating wings. A spear transfixed it, and it fell back. There followed in succession a dingo, a goanna, a snake, a frilled lizard, a crow, a magpie, and a wombat, each of which was killed and burnt.

At last the body of the Evil One collapsed into ashes amongst the embers.

'That is the end of the Evil One,' said the hermit.

'Wait!' the elder Winjarning warned. 'It may not be the end.'

They waited until the glow of the red embers faded and grey ashes lay on the ground. There was a slight movement. A caterpillar humped itself up and crawled across the sand. Winjarning stamped on it and threw it back. It sizzled and curled up in the heat. A centipede darted out, and met the same fate. A moth fluttered upwards and was caught with difficulty.

'The end?' asked the hermit when many hours had passed, and the last of the embers was barely visible in the darkness.

'Wait!'

Winjarning held a torch close to the ground and examined it carefully.

An ant was slowly threading its way between the stones and scattered blades of grass. Winjarning picked it up and placed it on the embers. Its body crackled and snapped, and dissolved, and the last ember winked out.

'The end!' Winjarning said with a sigh. 'The end of the Evil One!'

No longer can he take the form of any animal, or bird, or insect, or reptile, but alas! Winjarning overlooked Man. It is in the form of Man, and Man alone, that Marmoo the Evil One still appears, making trouble everywhere, and perpetuating evil in the world.

 The Keen Keengs and the Flame God

In the middle of the cave was a smooth, round hole, bleached white by fire. Beneath it slept the Flame God. A red light shone through the hole, staining the rocky walls with pink and lighting up the pallid features of a Keen Keeng, who tossed restlessly in sleep.

Another Keen Keeng, who had been out on reconnaissance, folded his wings and alighted at the entrance. He was a typical specimen of the strange race descended from the giants. He had to bend his head to enter the cave. When he straightened up, his wings were folded back in grooves that ran the length of his arms, and he had the appearance of a tall man, the only difference being that he had only two fingers and a thumb on each hand. The sleepers in the cave woke up and asked for news.

'There are two men on a bare plain many miles from here,' he said.

'Why didn't you bring them back with you?' they asked. 'We need men and women to offer to the Flame God when he wakes up. He is bound to be hungry, and if we have no sacrifice to offer, we will be seared by his anger.'

'There is a reason,' the scout replied. 'You are too impatient. They are no ordinary men: they are the Winjarning brothers!'

This statement silenced the Keen Keengs for several minutes. They well knew that the Winjarning brothers were the two most powerful wirinuns in all the land. Special gifts had been conferred on them by the Great Spirit, which enabled them to protect ordinary men and women from attacks by the non-human creatures who haunted desert and mountain. No one had ever appealed to the Winjarnings in vain. They had often saved their fellow men from Keen Keengs who tried to snatch them up as offerings to the Flame God. In consequence the descendants of the giants had suffered from the Flame God's anger.

'Did these men see you?' one of the older creatures asked, shuffling forward to warm his hands at the glowing hole in the floor.

'No; I flew at a great height, and only went low enough to see who they were. They did not lift their heads.'

'Then this may be the opportunity we have been waiting for. It is our chance to put an end to them, and to please the Flame God with a sacrifice that is worthy of him.'

'But they are too powerful for us to overcome,' someone objected.

The old Keen Keeng drew himself up and spoke more vigorously.

'Wisdom comes only to the aged,' he said. 'Listen to me. The Winjarning brothers have never seen us. They may have heard the beating of our wings in the darkness, but they have been too intent on saving others to notice us. Let us invite them to visit us. If we speak gentle words and show them we are friendly, their curiosity may be roused.'

Far across the plain the Winjarning wirinuns looked at each other and smiled. Their spirits had heard every word that had been spoken in the cave.

Presently they heard the beating of wings. A man-like figure appeared in the sky, grew larger, and landed on its feet in front of them.

'Who are you?' asked the older brother.

'Greetings! I am one of the Keen Keengs, who are the friends of everyone. I saw you from a great way off and have come to invite you to our home.'

The brothers appeared to consult together.

'Why should we go?' asked the younger one. 'We have heard strange tales about you. You are trying to trap us.'

'No, no,' the Keen Keeng replied earnestly. 'The sun is hot and there is no shade, no water to drink, no food here. Come with me and we will give you all these things and show you the mysteries and delights of the Keen Keengs.'

'Why should you do this for us? We are perfectly happy where we are.'

'We have heard about you. I know that your name is Winjarning, and that everyone respects you. Perhaps we will need your help some day.'

'Perhaps! How far is it to your home?'

'Many, many miles, but my wings are strong. I can carry you both on my back.'

'I should like to see the world as it looks to a bird,' said the younger brother. 'Let us go.'

They climbed on the Keen Keeng's back. He spread his wings and ran along the ground until he was airborne. His wings flapped and he rose swiftly from the ground with his heavy burden. Currents of warm air caused him to dip and sway as the wirinuns clung to his shoulders.

The Keen Keeng mounted higher. Fleecy clouds sailed by. Looking down, the wirinuns saw, as if from a mountain top, a flat plain with little dots and elongated shadows that were bushes. They saw the darker depressions of water holes, and far away a glint of silver at the foot of the mountain which, the Keen Keeng told them, was a lake close to his home.

Presently they were surrounded by other flying forms. These were the young Keen Keengs who had come to escort them. The distant mountain drew nearer, the lake passed under them, and they came to the mountain side and the black hole which was the entrance to the cave.

The brothers alighted and went inside. When their eyes grew accustomed to the dim light, they could see the older Keen Keengs ranged round the walls, and a very old man who advanced towards them and gave them a formal welcome. Then the younger Keen Keengs came jostling in, shouting and laughing. Food and water were put in front of the visitors, who were seated in the place of honour.

'Is this not a good place?' the oldest Keen Keeng asked. 'Here is shelter from the sun, protection from our enemies, and food and warmth.'

'We thought you were friends of everybody. How is it then that you have enemies?'

'There are wild beasts and creatures of the night,' the old one replied. 'But let us not think of unpleasant things. Sleep for a little while and then our young people will dance for you.'

For three days the Winjarning brothers were entertained by the Keen Keengs. They observed the dances of the young people closely, for they had never seen such rhythmic movement before. They memorised them, and in later years taught them to mankind, bequeathing to them the ritual of the dances that are used at the initiation rites of the young men and women who are verging on manhood and womanhood.

Each day the glow from the pit grew stronger. No one said anything and the brothers were careful to make no remark about it. The Keen Keengs knew that the Flame God was waking, and rejoiced that they had such a splendid offering to make to him.

'We must return to our camp now,' said one of the brothers. 'You have been hospitable to us, and we shall never forget your kindness, but now it is time for us to return and live our own lives.'

'Wait one more day,' the old Keen Keeng said. 'We have saved the best till last. Tonight the young women will perform the emu dance for you. You must not leave until you have seen it.'

A tongue of flame danced up out of the pit as though to emphasise his words.

'Very well, then. But tomorrow we must leave. That is our word.'

'You will not be sorry. After the emu dance there will be something you have never experienced before, nor will you ever see it again.'

The brother wirinuns went to the furthest corner of the cave and lay down as if they would sleep.

'This is the night,' whispered the elder brother. 'The last words were a warning that the old one thought we would not understand. Tonight we shall put an end to the wicked ways of the Keen Keengs, but we must be careful. When I whisper ''*Now!*'' you must leap to your feet and run out of the cave as swiftly as a hunting spear leaving the woomera.'

'Why?' protested the younger brother. 'I always take the lead in battle. Why should I run away?'

'Don't you remember what was said when we listened with our spirits? ''Wisdom comes to the aged'', were the words. I am not an old man, but I am older than you. It is your vigour and my wisdom working together that bring success. Alone they could accomplish nothing.'

'Very well,' the young brother replied, 'but I still don't know why you chose me for this part.'

They pretended to sleep, until they were roused by the old one.

'It is time now. The girls have assembled. You must not look at them, for it is a sacred dance that men are not allowed to see. Turn your backs and watch the wall of the cave.'

The brothers were fascinated by the dance that followed. Flames darted out of the pit, painting the walls blood-red. Silhouetted against the glowing panel were the black shadows of emus, who stretched their necks and leaped in the air, and made graceful movements with their wings.

Out of the corner of his eye the elder Winjarning saw other stealthy movements. The Keen Keengs were sidling round the walls below the shadows. There was a hiss and a roar that drowned the chant and the drums which accompanied the dance. Red and yellow flames shot up to the roof and flowered like waratah blossoms.

'*Now!*' shouted the elder brother.

The younger men darted forward and vanished through the entrance with the Keen Keeng men running after him. They lost him in the darkness and returned to the cave, to discover a strange sight. The elder Winjarning was dancing round the pit, with the appearance of blood and fire, and was followed by all the girls and the older women. He went so quickly that the females became dizzzy; one after another they fell sideways and dropped into the fiery pit of the Flame God.

Brandishing their weapons, the men ran to the attack, but they too were caught up in the furious dance that gyrated round the pit of death. It did not stop until the last Keen Keeng sacrificed himself involuntarily to his Flame God.

The young wirinun put his head round the entrance to see what was happening.

'Let us leave this place quickly,' said the older brother. 'The god is fed, but he has no worshippers. The place is accursed.'

They felt their way down the mountain side, skirted the lake, and walked across the plain. Sunlight was gilding the peak of the mountain when they looked back. It was like a tongue of living fire on the rocks. As they watched, the stones tumbled down and a long shaft of flame touched the sky. It sank, and was followed by a cloud of sparks which spun upwards until they were lost to sight. The mountain folded in on itself and settled down until there was nothing but bare flat plain as far as the eye could see.

The brothers returned cautiously, but all they could find were swarms of ants scuttling in and out of crevices in the ground.

That night they made their camp far away. The starry mantle of night was spread across the heavens.

'Look!' one of them exclaimed. 'The Keen Keengs! The sparks are still there, in the sky; they are telling us that the Flame God and his followers are dead.'

 ## The Dog-faced Man

Cheeroonear and his six hunting dogs were the scourge of the Nullarbor plain, but no one had ever seen them. It was only at the time of his death that the full horror of the Dog-man was realised. Up to the time of his capture, the man and wife and their evil dogs were but a story to frighten naughty children, or to cause backward glances when the shadows of the trees sprang frighteningly into the circle of firelight. Hunters who came across their tracks were puzzled by deep indentations made by human feet and marks that trailed beside them like the fingers of a hand. What had been most frightening of all was that no one had seen these grim monsters who snatched children, women, and men away, leaving only gnawed bones to bear witness that they had been living people.

There came a summer of intense drought. Leaves drooped limply from the trees, and the land was scorched to cinders and dry earth. Water holes steamed in the sun, and soon dried up. Nothing moved under that burning sky. Human beings had taken shelter near the top of a hill above the last water hole, which was shaded by rocks and bushes; snakes, birds, and animals huddled close to them on the steep hillside.

'What is that?' an old woman croaked, trying in vain to moisten her lips.

The people feebly lifted their heads; with bloodshot eyes they gazed out across the plain. They were too weary to show interest. But one, more active than the others, kept watch. Suddenly he gave a cry of horror. A solitary figure had reached the bottom of the hill and was climbing up towards the water hole. The hair rose on every scalp, for as he came closer men saw such a sight as they had never seen before. The figure was tall and heavily built, with the arms and legs of a man, but his head and ears were those of a dog. From his mouth and chin hung a loose bag like that of a pelican. It was deflated, and the loose folds swung in a hollow in his chest. His arms were unnaturally long, and as he walked they swung to and fro, trailing along the ground. By this the hunters who had sometimes seen his tracks in the sandy soil knew that he must be Cheeroonear.

The Dog-man walked past them to the water hole. As he drank, the bag in his chest began to swell out like a ball, the skin became swollen and distended. He was so thirsty that he gulped the water, careless of the consequences of over-indulgence. Hardly had he taken more than a dozen steps down the hill than he was sick, vomiting water and food which contained human bones and skulls. He turned savagely towards the petrified onlookers and said in a deep, distorted voice, 'Now you have seen Cheeroonear; but you shall not live to tell the tale. Long ago it was foretold that if ever I were seen by men and women my death would follow quickly. You have seen me; but I shall wipe out your memories before another sun rises, I, and my wife, and my dogs.'

Before the men could reach for their weapons, he plunged off down the hillside, running with great strides which soon carried him across the plain and out of sight.

'Alas, what shall we do?' wailed the old woman who had first seen him.

'Lie in wait for him and kill him when he returns,' suggested one of the younger men, and his companions agreed.

'Wait a moment,' a wise old hunter counselled. 'This is no matter for hasty decision. You think you can kill him; but what of his dogs?'

'We shall kill them too.'

'And his wife?'

'Kill, kill!'

'It needs more skill than you seem to think. Remember, Cheeroonear has never been seen until today. It was not carelessness that revealed him to us, but the urgent need for water—a need that has brought animals and reptiles and men together. This is a strange day that will be remembered long after our spirits have left our bodies. Do you think that Cheeroonear has lost the skill to snatch us one by one in the dark? Can you tell where he will come from, he, and his wife, and his dogs? How will you protect your women and children? And where will you be when death melts like a shadow under the trees, darker than night itself?'

'What else can we do?' they asked sulkily. 'We must defend ourselves.'

'You can try to do that; but if you are as sensible as you appear to be brave, you will seek for help.'

'Who will help us?'

'The Winjarning brothers, who respond to every appeal that is made to them. The time has come for you to bury your pride.'

The young man consulted among themselves and agreed that the old hunter had counselled wisely. They made a swift journey to the sea, in spite of the heat, and told the Winjarnings of the plight of their tribe.

'We shall come,' was the answer. 'Take the word back to your people, and tell them not to be afraid. The ancient prophesy that when Cheeroonear is seen by men he will meet his death will come true. Expect us when the moon is at its zenith.'

At midnight on the night of full moon the bushes parted and the wirinuns walked into the camp.

'Wake up, friends,' they said. 'There is work to be done.'

The people gathered round them eagerly.

'Let the young men stand over here.'

The brothers looked at them and counted them, and said, 'There are enough of you to do what we want. And you have the moon to help you. Go down the hill and gather as much brushwood as you can. Bring it back here and we shall show you where to put it.'

The young men brought piles of brushwood so large that they looked like ants walking underneath them.

The light wood was laid in two long rows hundreds of yards in length, making a path that led to the water hole, and converging to a narrow exit.

'It will be like a kangaroo hunt,' the Winjarnings explained.

As the sky began to grow light in the east, the warriors were given their orders.

'Take your weapons and stand behind the barricades. If any of the dogs break through, you know what to do; but if they keep to the path we have made for them, leave them to us.'

The women and children were sent off to hiding places among the rocks. Everybody was now in position. A silence hung over the hill and the plain; birds and animals were mute as the light grew stronger. A little breeze lifted over the hill, stirred the leaves, and died away again. From far away came the barking of a pack of dogs.

The light was strong enough for the waiting men to see them as they ran up the hill. The dogs were running silently. They stood nearly as high as a man at the shoulder, and there was something blood-chilling as they ran with loping strides, their paws padding softly on the hard ground. Sharp white teeth glistened in their open mouths. One after the other they passed through the bushes and on to the long path bordered by masses of brushwood, between the motionless warriors whose spears and clubs were lifted in the air.

The first dog reached the end of the path and stopped, his muzzle lifted high, his eyes blazing. One of the Winjarning brothers brought his boomerang down and severed the head from its body. He kicked the head to one side and dragged the body clear of the track. The next dog bounded through, and the second Winjarning struck off its head and tossed the body back to one of the warriors. Unsuspectingly the dogs rushed to their doom, and a few moments later the bloodied boomerangs were lowered; six heads and six bodies lay severed on the ground.

The brothers took flint knives from their belts and cut off the dogs' tails, handing them to one of the warriors who had been given special instructions. The silence fell once more. No one moved or spoke. Time stood still while man and beast, bird and reptile and insect waited for what was yet to come. The sun leaped over the hill and mounted into the sky.

Now a hoarse panting broke the silence. Cheeroonear was tired of waiting for his dogs to return and had come up to see what had happened to them. He pulled himself over the rocks with his long arms. The Winjarnings prayed to the Great Spirit, and the hilltop was wreathed in mist. Women and girls wailed as though in mortal fear, and amongst the low bushes six warriors danced and whisked the tails of the dogs so that Cheeroonear believed his dogs were hunting human quarry.

The Dog-man chuckled deep in his throat and raced along the track to help them.

'It is Cheeroonear who has come to kill you,' he shouted. 'Tremble, you little people, and look your last on the red sun.'

His pouch at his throat throbbed and distended in anticipation of the coming feast. He reached the end of the trail. Out of the mist the waddies of the brothers crashed on to his head and struck him spinning to the ground, his arms flailing, his long claw-like hands clutching for the prey he could not find. Again and again the clubs descended until his body lay lifeless on the rocks, with one hand grasping a stone at the edge of the water hole.

The warriors relaxed and women began to emerge from their hiding places; but the brothers whispered a warning.

'Back! The danger is not over yet. Back to your places, warriors and women!'

The men stiffened and returned to their places, the women scrambled back into hiding. The silent vigil began again. Without warning another figure loomed through the mist: it was Cheeroonear's wife. She stood still and listened, but there was no sound to break the silence. She crept stealthily along the path. When the men had seen Cheeroonear they had tightened the grip on their weapons; but at the sight of this woman they shut their eyes for they dared not look at her. Slowly she advanced, step by step, peering into the fog, her ears pricked to catch the smallest sound. Her swollen sides brushed against the bushes. At the end of the path she saw the body of her husband.

The nearest warriors fell on her and hacked her body in two. Then from every tree and from behind every bush rushed the exultant men and women of the tribe.

The two halves of the body twitched. From the upper part emerged a boy. The men recovered quickly from their astonishment and ran towards him, but he changed into a reptile that escaped from under their feet.

Cheeroonear was dead; the six dogs were dead; the woman was dead; but the devil that came from her body is alive in the bush—today!

 The Jealous Twins

The twins Perindi and Harrimiah were renowned as an example of brotherly love. No quarrels ever marred their affection: they played together as boys, went through their initiation test together and, as young warriors and hunters, worked together as a team. Each esteemed the other more than himself and was proud of his brother's prowess.

Scheming uncles sought them as husbands for their nieces, but Perindi and Harrimiah were satisfied with their own company. They took no notice of the girls who tried to attract their attention, and it seemed as though they might never marry lest their friendship should be broken by women.

Much as they admired the twins, the elders of the tribe were concerned about this.

'It is not natural that two men should live together and not take wives for themselves,' grumbled an elder in the council meeting. 'It is only what you would expect of twins.'

'Don't worry,' laughed another. 'The girls will soon plan something.'

'Then it will be a good thing, as long as they do not offend against our customs.'

'The twins will never know what has happened to them,' replied the second speaker. 'The wiles of women are beyond the understanding of men. The tribal games will soon begin, and we shall see what will happen.'

Perindi and Harrimiah took part in the contests. They made their encampment at a little distance from the others, but mingled with the excited young men and women during the day. Sometimes they were separated, and on one of these occasions Perindi met a young woman who had many interesting things to tell him about himself. She said little or nothing about Harrimiah, but she spoke in glowing words of Perindi's physique and appearance, of his prowess as a hunter, and his wisdom.

'All we girls admire you,' she said before they parted, 'but some of them keep talking about your brother. He has been boasting that he is braver and more skilful than you, and better-looking too. So don't let him overshadow you in the games. Some of the girls expect that he will make you take second place to him tomorrow.'

Perindi went home in thoughtful mood. He could not think of anything that Harrimiah had done to belittle him in any way, but dark suspicions flitted batlike through his mind. They did not disappear during the night, but grew darker and stronger than ever.

'I must teach my brother a lesson he will not quickly forget,' he thought.

'Come, Harrimiah, we must prepare ourselves for the corroboree,' he said in a loud and cheerful voice. 'Let me paint your body.'

'No, I will do yours first,' said Harrimiah, for he dearly wished to see how handsome his brother would look when he was painted.

He took white clay and yellow ochre, and carefully drew circles and spirals, broad bands and wavy lines on his brother's dark body. Standing back to admire his work, he felt that he had done justice to his greatly loved brother.

Perindi felt a moment of remorse. His brother seemed so genuinely interested in seeing that he made a brave show at the games. Then he remembered what the girl had told him and his heart hardened.

'Now I will adorn you, brother,' he said. 'I will put charcoal on you first to make a background for the pattern.'

He smeared Harrimiah with charcoal from head to foot, and painted the patterns, but he made them smudged and indistinct, and they did not stand out clearly.

As they walked towards the main encampment, they were greeted by the young women who came out to meet them. Most of them ran up to Perindi. They surrounded him and bore him away, exclaiming with admiration at the beautiful colours and designs with which he was decorated. A few remained with Harrimiah, but they giggled, as young women often do, and spoke to each other in whispers. Harrimiah was puzzled. He looked across and saw his brother in the centre of a large and admiring throng of girls.

'Is there something the matter with me?' he asked. 'What are you laughing at?'

'Nothing, nothing,' they assured him, and ran off to join the others.

Harrimiah shook his head in a puzzled manner and sat down by the edge of a pool, wondering why he had been deserted. He was glad that his brother was so popular, and he had no envy in his heart; yet it was strange that the girls should take no notice of him, because it was usual for them to divide their favours equally.

He bent over the pool to drink. When he saw his reflection in the water his eyes narrowed. No wonder the girls had laughed at him! He looked as drab as a crow in his dowdy plumage.

'Perindi is no good at painting,' he said aloud. 'I did the best I could and everyone is admiring him. I wonder what has happened.'

He rose and made his way across to his brother.

'Come on, Perindi,' he said. 'The girls are in a foolish mood this morning. Leave them and we will take our part in the games together.'

'The girls have been admiring the designs on my body, Harrimiah. Now let us see how we can perform in the dances.'

'Why did you paint me so badly, Perindi?'

'There's nothing wrong with my painting, brother. Perhaps it is because I have a better body than you that everyone is attracted to me today. But let's see what happens in the dances. I'm certainly a better dancer than you.'

Harrimiah was downcast as they walked together. It was the first time there had been any suggestion of competition between them.

In spite of Perindi's boastful words, it was difficult to tell which was the better dancer of the two; that they were both more skilful than all the other young men was never in doubt.

In the wurley that night the brothers had little to say to each other; Perindi was sulky and quarrelsome.

The following morning they were called on to perform the frog dance. Perindi was again admired for his skilful ornamentation, but when the performance was over a number of the girls flocked round Harrimiah and flattered him, loudly praising the energy and grace of his dancing. Perindi frowned. Something seemed to break inside him, and he was consumed with anger as though a fire had been lit in his bowels.

He shouted at his brother.

'I am through with you. From now on you can go your own way and do what you like; but if ever I see you again I will put my spear through your heart!'

He strode off and made a new camp for himself far away from the hunting grounds he had shared with his brother. In the course of time young women became attractive to him, and he married a girl of the Blue-tongued Lizard totem. Harrimiah grieved for a long time. The love he had felt for his brother was not something that could be wiped out in a single day. He suspected that it was the flattery of the women that had turned Perindi against him.

It was lonely living alone. When he heard of Perindi's marriage he realised that there was no hope of reconciliation. He chose an attractive young woman of the Frilled Lizard totem and settled down to married life, discovering that the devotion of a woman who needed protection was even better than affection shared with a brother.

'Perhaps it has all turned out for the best,' he was thinking one day when he was out hunting for wallabies. He saw a movement behind a bush and crept round it warily, to find himself looking into his brother's eyes.

'Perindi!' he cried.

Perindi's eyes blazed like flaming coals. He leaped on Harrimiah and fastened his teeth in his throat, tearing the skin from his neck.

Unseen by either of the brothers, their families had drawn near to the scene of the fight. They pulled them apart and led Harrimiah away. His wife bathed his lacerated neck and applied a poultice of ashes of mulga wood. The wound healed, but it left an ugly scar which can still be seen on the neck of the Lace Lizard.

Perindi's vicious treatment of his brother antagonised his own wife and her relatives. They even drove him out of their camp; he took to the bush and developed peculiar habits.

Harrimiah's life was changed, too. He had never ceased to love his brother in spite of all that Perindi had done to him. He spent much of his time away from his camp, sleeping alone under the stars. Birds and reptiles, trees and bushes, sorrowed with him in his grief, and their anger against Perindi grew deeper. For Harrimiah the trees lowered their branches to shield him from the burning sun, and the birds sang their sweetest; but to Perindi the trees denied their shade and the birds sang no song. Perindi's heart was like a stone; but his twin felt that his would melt in sorrow.

The birds urged him to take revenge, and promised their support. The trees offered their wood for spears, and snakes their poison fangs, but Harrimiah kept on repeating that the only help he needed was in winning back the love of Perindi.

The hopes that he had cherished began at length to fade. Wearily he dug a pit underneath a wattle and a wild apple tree, and lay down in it. The night wind blew the sand over him and he slept. His tears were swallowed by the thirsty earth, which in return gave him peace and rest.

Harrimiah's wife was heart-broken at his long absence. She gathered her friends together and they followed his trail. It wound through the bush and across the empty sands, coming to an end by the shallow grave, which was guarded by a solitary crow.

'Harrimiah is sleeping,' the crow told them. 'It is the end of his grief. He loves you all—wife, relatives, and brother; but life was not big enough to contain his sorrow. Let him rest. In sleep he forgets.'

'He will forget,' said his wife. 'Peace will come to him in sleep, and when he wakes it will be to the joy of another life.'

She begged the apple and wattle trees to receive her spirit and to take the spirits of all her people. The trees embraced them, and continued to stand patiently beside the grave of Harrimiah.

When they bloom he will rise from his grave to new life, and the spirits of his wife and her people will emerge from the sheltering trees and join him in a new world where jealousy and grief are never to be found.

The Dog Owners

Of Newal and his wife and dog it was hard to say which was the most heartless. They lived together in a hollow tree with only one entrance, several feet from the ground. Their access was by means of a log which leaned against the trunk. All three were flesh-eaters, and they enjoyed all kinds of meat except birds.

Their favourite food was human flesh. They had such a craving for it that a great deal of their time was spent lying in ambush trying to capture unwary hunters. At this they became so successful that tribes for many miles round began to grow anxious. Many of their finest warriors and hunters disappeared and were never seen again; no one could tell what had happened to them.

Newal and his dog grew over-confident, and so suffered a shock that taught them a lesson. They were hiding in thick scrub one day when they saw two hunters coming towards them. A kangaroo was feeding close by. The hunters saw it and began to stalk the animal, crawling from bush to bush, getting closer to Newal all the time. He whispered in the dog's ear.

'They will pass between us and the bush over there. Be ready!'

Before long the men were crouching under the very bush which Newal had chosen to hide behind. Both man and dop leaped at them, one with uplifted spear and the other with bared teeth; but these hunters were quick-witted and agile—they snatched their nullanullas and belaboured man and dog until they fled. As one man, the hunters picked up their boomerangs and threw them. The first inflicted a gash in Newal's arm, the second severed the dog's tail at the root.

It was an unhappy man and dog who climbed up the sloping log to the tree house that night. Their wounds took a long time to heal and kept them from hunting. Newal's wife did what she could, but she was only a woman and unskilled in hunting. The only provisions she could gather were roots and grubs. It was many weeks before the man and dog recovered.

'We are weak from lack of good red meat,' said Newal to his wife. 'Today the dog and I go hunting. Wallaby meat, kangaroo meat, wombat meat will not satisfy me. I need the flesh of man.'

He set off with his dog. In the distance they espied a band of young men hunting emus.

'Let us cut one of them off,' said the dog.

They advanced stealthily under cover of the scrub, but the sharp-eyed hunters saw the bushes moving and came over to investigate.

'It is Newal and his dog,' they shouted, because the news of the man and his dog had become widely known while they were recovering from their wounds. They set off after them and pursued them so hotly that they barely escaped with their lives.

A solemn discussion was held in the hollow tree that night. Newal had been badly scared.

'The whole trouble is that we were seen by the men who wounded us,' he said. 'Everyone is on the lookout for us now, and we are too easily recognised. From now on we will have to satisfy ourselves with animal meat. When we can't get that we may even have to eat the flesh of birds.'

The other two set up a howl of protest.

'You give up far too easily,' the dog told his master. 'If you can't get what you want by force, you must use guile. We must not be seen together, but you can get what we want by yourself.'

'By myself!' Newal exclaimed. 'Why should I have all the work to do?'

'Don't be upset. I will play my part. You must go out and walk through the bush until you meet a solitary hunter. Choose one who has walked a long way and is tired and thirsty. Tell him to come to your home where he may rest and refresh himself.'

'That is right,' the woman said. 'We cannot live without human food, and that is how you can get it.'

So the following morning Newal set out by himself, grumbling as he went. In the late afternoon he met a hunter and spoke to him ingratiatingly.

'You look tired. Have you come a long way?'

'You can see that for yourself,' the hunter answered shortly. 'A man does not catch kangaroos easily or quickly.'

'You have a long walk before you reach your camp?'

'Yes.'

'Then come with me to my home. It is only a little way off. You can rest there and enjoy the coldest water you ever drank. It bubbles from an underground spring inside a hollow tree, and there I live with my family.'

The hunter was curious, never having heard of such a thing before, and accompanied Newal to the tree.

'Stay a moment,' Newal ordered. He ran up the log and put his head through the entrance.

'Here is our supper,' he whispered excitedly. 'Are you ready?'

'Ready,' growled the dog.

'Ready,' grinned the wife.

Newal returned to the hunter.

'All is well. Leave your burden here. Go up the sloping log and put your head through the hole in the tree and look down. There you will see something you will never forget.'

The hunter climbed the log, put his hands on the tree trunk, and thrust his head through the hole. The dog sprang at him and sank his teeth in the man's neck, while Newal's wife struck him heavily on the head with her club. His body slid down and fell lifeless at the foot of the tree.

'See how simple it is,' the dog barked as he bounded out of the tree and scampered down the log.

'Hurry, woman. Light the fire. It is two moons since I tasted human flesh.'

The experiment had been so successful that it was repeated many times. Once more word went from tribe to tribe that some hidden danger lurked in the bush; but no one was able to discover what form it took until one day two strangers arrived in that part of the country. They were tall men and walked with dignity. Everyone made them welcome, and they talked to their hosts until far into the night, telling of the wonderful sights they had seen in their travels. No one dared to ask their names, though there were some who whispered to each other that they might be the Winjarning brothers who had come to do justice.

It was an old man nodding over the fire who discovered the truth. He was dreaming of sights he had seen many years before when a memory rose out of the past. He stood up and in a quavering voice said, 'This is Buda Gooda, and this is his brother.'

Other men sprang to their feet looking expectantly at the strangers.

'Yes,' said the older brother, 'you have guessed aright. We have heard of your troubles and have come to see whether we can help you.'

Tongues were loosened. The visitors were told of the many hunters who had been lost, and how no man knew what had happened to them.

'We will go out tomorrow and will see what will befall,' Buda Gooda and his brother promised.

Newal met them some miles from the encampment.

'You look hot and tired,' he said.

'Yes,' Buda Gooda replied, not knowing that this was the man he was seeking. 'We did not bring water bags with us and we are thirsty. Do you know where we can find a water hole?'

'I can do better than that,' Newal replied. 'My home is not far away. It is in a hollow tree in which there is a spring of pure water that bubbles up from the depths of the earth. You are welcome to come and satisfy your thirst.'

The brothers went with him.

'Wait here,' Newal said to the younger brother. 'My wife is a little nervous and will be afraid if two strangers enter her home at once.'

Buda Gooda accompanied Newal. In his bones he felt that there was something curious and a little sinister about the man.

'Wait by this tree,' Newal said to his guest. 'My home is in the hollow tree over there. I will tell my wife that you are coming.'

He walked over to the tree, climbed the log, and went inside to prepare his wife and the dog to receive two separate meals. As soon as he was out of sight Buda Gooda tiptoed forward and looked round the camp fire. The ground was covered with skulls and human bones. His brother followed him and hid behind a tree.

Newal returned.

'All is ready,' he announced. 'Come, climb up the log, and put your head inside the opening. You will see something you will never forget as long as you live.'

Buda Gooda went slowly up the log ramp. Before he put his head through the hole he held his parrying shield in front of him. Inside the tree the dog saw the man's head appear. He sprang at his throat, but his teeth sank into the wood of the shield, and he could not let go. Newal's wife struck at Buda Gooda's head, but he caught the club, wrenched it from her hand, and brought it down with such force that her skull was crushed. The dog was still hanging on to the shield. Buda Gooda dashed it against the side of the tree, but as he was doing this, Newal sprang on to the log and swung his nullanulla in a terrific blow directed at the base of Buda's skull.

The nullanulla was poised high above Newal's head when a searing flash of light seemed to pass through him and he fell lifeless from the log. Buda Gooda's brother had fitted a spear to his woomera and sent it whistling through the air to lodge in the heart of the last of the eaters of human flesh.

 ## Mummulbery and Thardid Jimbo

There were few giants in Australia. The greatest of all was the mother of the dwarf Woo, whose tear-channelled sides are seen in Mount Gambier. Thardid Jimbo was only seven feet tall ... but a man of this height is surely a giant among other men. It was a sad day for Mummulbery when he met Thardid Jimbo.

Mummulbery was the gentlest of men. He went his own way and preferred to make his camp far from the rest of his tribe. He had two wives. Being young women, it might be thought that they would have preferred the company of girls of their own age, but they took delight in looking after their man. They were sisters.

The tiny encampment often rang with happy laughter. It was only when all three were together that they felt that their lives were complete; but as they depended on the strong arm of Mummulbery for meat and the industry of the girls for vegetable foods, it was necessary for them to separate during the day. The loneliness of the daylight hours was always compensated by the reunion round the fire in the evenings, and the long hours of darkness were enlivened by the comforting glow of the fires and the sleepy talk in which the day's adventures were gaily related.

One day Mummulbery came upon the fresh trail of a kangaroo. It was a powerful beast and by the time he caught up with it, he had strayed far from his usual hunting grounds. Mummulbery thrust the butt of a long pole into the ground. To the other end he had fastened the wings of an eagle-hawk. He shook the pole vigorously until the wings flapped like those of a bird in flight. The kangaroo stopped to investigate. While its attention was occupied, the hunter crept close to it and clubbed the animal to death before it was even aware of his presence.

Mummulbery picked up his weapons, slung the animal across his shoulders, and turned, to find himself face to face with Thardid Jimbo. The giant, who liked human flesh as a change in his diet, had picked up the hunter's trail and had been following him. Mummulbery was startled, but he spoke words of cordial greeting. A broad grin spread over Thardid Jimbo's face.

'Greetings to you, hunter. I followed you to see whether you were a man of skill, and I see you are. That is a fine kangaroo.'

'Yes,' agreed Mummulbery. 'It will be better still when its flesh is roasted. I have plenty of meat now. Would you like some?'

'I am rather particular about my food. Come closer so that I can examine it. Now turn round. I can only see the head and legs, the way you are holding it.'

Mummulbery turned round for the giant to inspect the body. As swift as lightning Thardid Jimbo severed the hunter's head from his body with a single snap of his strong teeth. He kindled a fire, cooked Mummulbery's limbs, and sat down to eat. It was a huge meal, as befitted a giant: flesh, skin, and bones, all went into his capacious belly. The body was left. He tucked it under his arm and followed Mummulbery's trail back to his camp. His long legs carried him quickly over the ground, and he arrived just as the young women were returning with the day's supply of yams.

They looked up, ready to greet their husband. It was a fearful shock to see the bushes part and Thardid Jimbo's body looming over them. He threw his burden on the ground before them and said, 'I am hungry. Hurry up and cook the meat for me.'

Their hands flew to their mouths to suppress a scream, for they had recognised the body of their dearly loved husband. But they stood their ground, for Mummulbery had trained them to be resourceful and self-reliant.

'If anything ever happens to me, I want you to be able to look after yourselves,' he had often told them. 'My brothers would doubtless be ready to marry you if I died, but remember that you see little of your families.

You would have to support yourselves during the year of mourning, and I would not like you to be frightened or to go hungry.'

They looked at the poor, helpless body and remembered what he had told them.

'We are hungry too,' they said. 'We will cook a meal for you, but we cannot eat human flesh. You can save the body for another time.'

'Very well,' Thardid Jimbo replied. 'I don't mind what it is so long as it's meat. But hurry up. I am going to take you for my wives because you are fine girls. We will be leaving the camp soon, and we have a long way to go.'

'We would be proud to be the wives of such a man as you,' said the elder sister. 'For the first meal to celebrate our new life we would like you to kill something specially for us.'

The giant was much flattered by the interest the girls showed in him. 'What do you want?' he asked.

'In the cave you can see from here there lives a dingo. It is a long time since we had a meal of dingo meat.'

Taking his nullanulla with him, Thardid Jimbo strode off and entered the cave. It was some little time before he returned, carrying an armful of puppies.

'Are these what you want?'

'Oh no. Pups are no good. It's the mother dingo we want.'

'I didn't see one there.'

'You will have to go right to the far end of the cave.'

'A foolish woman's whim,' he grumbled, but he went back again.

It was a deep cave. The women knew it would take Thardid Jimbo a long time to go to the end and come back. They gathered armfuls of scrub, piled it up at the entrance till it touched the roof, and set fire to it. The wind carried the smoke into the cave, while the branches crackled and burned furiously. Before long the girls heard the giant coughing and spluttering. The scrub had settled down and was burning fiercely by this time. Thardid Jimbo appeared out of the smoke, begrimed, with red eyes and singed hair, and very furiously angry. He flung his nullanulla at them, but missed. Taking a short run he attempted to jump over the fire; but he had forgotten his height. His head met the rock roof of the cave with a sickening thud, and he dropped unconscious into the fire. There he lay still, and the spirit left his charred flesh.

The danger was over now, but the girls had time to remember their grief. They sat with their arms round each other while the tears rolled down their cheeks. Night and day passed unheeded, for they neither ate nor slept.

Eventually the sharpness of sorrow was blunted, and they were ready to face the future.

'We must ask our father to come and help us,' they decided.

So they lit a fire and sent up a smoke signal. Before long an answering column rose from their parents' home. The next day their father arrived, and they showed him the pathetic remnant of Mummulbery's body, laid reverently on a pile of green leaves and branches.

'That is all that is left of our dear husband,' they wailed. 'He was killed by the wicked Thardid Jimbo. Oh father, can you not bring him back to us?'

'As a wirinun I have great power,' their father said gently, 'and there is much that I can do for you, my daughters; but to bring the spirit back into the mutilated body of a man is more than anyone could or should attempt. Of what use would a headless, limbless husband be to you? His spirit is happy, clothed in radiant flesh. Is your love for Mummulbery so great that you are willing to throw your earthly bodies away and join him?'

The hope that shone in their eyes was sufficient answer.

'Then let me embrace you for the last time,' he said.

The wirinun spoke mystic words and pleaded with the Great Spirit who rules the destinies of his children, begging him to restore his daughters to their husband.

Silence fell, a silence unbroken by the song of bird or insect, or even by the rustling of a leaf, as though the world were waiting for another day to begin. Then before them stood the spirit of Mummulbery, clothed in the flesh that had been so warm and satisfying in days gone by. He embraced his wives, reached out a hand to their father as though in blessing, and mounted up with them into the sky. Their bodies dwindled and were lost to sight in the infinite hunting grounds of the sky while they also remained standing by the cast-off flesh of their husband.

The sorrowful father buried their earthly bodies, and said to himself, 'Their light will never stop shining!' and he went off to tell his wife all that had happened.

Glossary

Bahloo: the moon god

Baiame: the Great Spirit

Baiamul: black swan

Bibbi: woodpecker

Bilbie: rabbit-eared bandicoot

billabong: isolated river pool

Birra-nulu: wife of Baiame

boomerang: throwing weapon

Booran: pelican

bora: initiation ceremony

Brolga: native companion

Bullima: spirit world

Bu-maya-mul: wood lizard

bunyip: monster of the swamp

Bunyun-bunyun: frog

Butterga: flying squirrel

Cheeroonear: dog-faced man

churinga: bullroarer (and other
  sacred objects)

coolabah: tree

coolamon: wooden drinking vessel

Deegeenboya: soldier bird

Deereeree: willy wagtail

dilly: string bag for carrying
  possessions

Dinewan: emu

Du-mer: brown pigeon

Eer-moonan: monsters

Ga-ra-gah: blue crane

Gidgeereegah: budgerigar or
  warbling grass parrot

Googoorewon: the place of trees

Goomblegubbon: bustard or brush
  turkey

Goonaroo: whistling duck, wife of
  Narahdarn and daughter of Bilbie

Goorgourgahgah: kookaburra

gunyah: hut

Gurangatch: water monster

humpy: hut

In-nard-dooah: porcupine

Keen Keengs: flying men descended
  from giants

Kinie-ger: native cat

Kubbitha: black duck, wife of
  Mungoongarlie

Kunnan-beili: wife of Baiame

kurria: crocodile guardian

Madhi: dog

Maira: paddy-melon

maldape: monster

mallee: eucalypt scrub

Marmoo: spirit of evil

Mar-rallang: wives of Wyun-gare

Meamei: the Pleiades, the Seven
  Sisters

miamia: hut

Millin-nulu-nubba: small bird

mingga: a spirit

Mirragen: cat

Mirram: kangaroo

Moodai: possum

Moograbah: bell magpie

Mullian: eagle-hawk

Mullian-ga: morning star, leader of the Mullians

Mungoongarlie: giant goanna

Murga-muggai: trapdoor spider

Murra-wunda: climbing rat

Narahdarn: bat

Nepelle: ruler of the heavens

Noyang: eel

nullanulla: club

Nungeena: mother spirit

Nurunderi: servant of Nepelle

Ooboon: blue-tongued lizard

Ouyarh: cockatoo

Ouyouboolooey: black snake

Pinyali: emu

Puckowie: the grandmother spirit

Pun-jel: spirit who rules in Milky Way with Baiame

Theen-who-ween: ancient name for emu

Tuckonies: tree spirits, or spirits of growth

tukkeri: fish forbidden to women

Tya: the earth

Wahlillie: wife of Narahdarn and daughter of Bilbie

Wahn: crow

Walla-gudjail-uan: spirit of birth

Walla-guroon-buan: a spirit

Warreen: wombat

Wayambeh: tortoise

Whowhie: monster of the Murray River

willywilly: whirlwind

wirinun: medicine man or priest

wirrie: stick to extract poison from dead body

Woggoon: mallee fowl

woomera: throwing stick

Wunda: evil spirit

Wungghee: mopoke

wurley: hut

Wurrawilberoo: whirlwind or whirlwind devil

Wyungare: 'he who returns to the stars'

yacca: grass tree

yaraan: a tree

Yara-ma-yha-who: a monster

Yarrageh: spirit of spring

Yee-na-pah: mountain devil

Yhi: sun goddess

They agreed. When autumn came the grubs and insects burrowed into the soil, crawled up the tree trunks, and hid in crevices in the bark, or swam under water and clung to the stalks of water-plants.

But no one had really taken them seriously. It was a long cold winter. Some of the birds had flown away to warmer lands, and anyone who remained was so busy keeping warm and seeking food that he forgot all about the bravery of the insect people. Snake, Wombat, Goanna, and Bandicoot were fast asleep, for they had found that it was an easy way to survive the rigours of the winter season.

Yarrageh had scarcely begun another season's labour of love when the Swifts came flying down to earth, chirping, excitedly, and calling the animals and birds together.

'We have seen something new, something new,' they sang. 'We have followed the path of Yarrageh, and now he has come to you, to you, to you.'

The animals gathered together expectantly. Presently they saw little moving specks of colour on the ground. They were the tribe of Beetles, resplendent in flashing metallic armour. Then a sharp-eyed bird saw a grey chrysalis hanging from a tree. The chrysalis opened, a butterfly emerged, and spread its delicate wings, fanning them slowly to and fro as if to dry them in the warm breeze. Something climbed out of the river and hung from a swaying stem. Wings, almost transparent, gradually unfolded and a long shining body stiffened and came to life in the sunshine. With a whirr of wings it flew up, hovering like a rainbow above them.

Butterflies and moths and insects of every shape and size, resplendent in their new dress, fluttered and swooped and ran among the birds and animals.

'So it is true,' Wahn shouted triumphantly. 'These are new insects. They have been born again with new spirits and new bodies. There *is* another world, and they have come to tell us that death is not the end of life.'

This was the miracle of spring; the miracle that returns every year when Yarrageh comes with warm, gentle breezes and fingers gay with colour.

The Digging Bone

In the Northern Territory, where a gulf bites deeply into the land, lagoons and marshes once extended far inland. They teemed with wildfowl, and on the drier parts animals were to be found everywhere. The birds and the animals lived happily together; there was plenty of food, and they were content to share the beautiful earth and water. But with the passing years the birds became jealous of the animals and lizards who came to the edge of the lagoons to drink, and who dared to swim in the water the birds regarded as their own.

'From now on you must keep to your own place,' said the birds. 'There is plenty of room for you on the land. If you are thirsty you can drink from the streams and the small pools, but you must leave the marshes to us. They are our homes. We build our nests there. You trample our grass, and you crush our reeds, and you dirty our water. Keep to your own place.'

The animals and lizards resented being ordered away from the lagoons which they regarded as their home just as much as the dry land.

'There is plenty of room for everyone in the marshes,' they complained, 'and there is very little dry land. It will be overcrowded if we have to stay there. We'll begin to fight among ourselves if we are not allowed to roam where we want. We have just as much right to the marshes and the lagoons as you.'

'Keep out! Keep out!' screamed the birds. 'They are ours, not yours. Keep out!'

Then the animals and lizards banded together. They advanced on the lagoons like an army, swarming on the edges, breaking down the reeds, treading unwittingly on the nests of the wildfowl. The birds rose up in clouds and attacked them with beak and claw. The air was thick with flying feathers, and fur, skin, scales, and blood floated across the marsh water.

The battle seemed to go on endlessly. Hundreds of birds and creatures of the land rose to take the place of those who were killed. From every part of the marshes hoarse shouts, high-pitched screaming, angry roaring, and the clash of weapons indicated that the fighting would never stop until all the living creatures were dead.

The only ones who took no part in the quarrel were Kangaroo, Emu, and Willy Wagtail. They met together and camped as far as they could from the contestants, but they could still hear the uproar of battle and the distant screams.

'We must do something to stop this bloodshed,' said Mirram the Kangaroo. 'It is sheer selfishness that has brought these troubles on us.'

'I am a bird, but I am ashamed of my people,' said Deereeree the Willy Wagtail sadly. 'Selfishness is deep inside us. I don't know how we can take it out.'

'Fighting won't do it.'

'Ah, but there is one thing that can be done. If we could take the marsh lands away from the birds there would be nothing left to fight over.'

'But what would happen to the birds?'

'They would find another place somewhere.'

'How could we possibly take the marsh lands away from them? There are only three of us. Even if we were as many as the reeds in all the lagoons, we would only cause more fighting, and that is just what we want to avoid.'

'There is one way we could do it,' Deereeree said excitedly. 'If we could let the sea into the lagoons, the birds would be left without a home. That would bring them to their senses.'

Dinewan the Emu spoke for the first time. 'Yes, that's all we would have to do,' he remarked sarcastically. 'Perhaps you can scratch a channel with your little claws, Deereeree?'

The bird hung its head, and Kangaroo rebuked Emu.

'If we quarrel amongst ourselves, Dinewan, nothing will be done. Let's build a shelter and go to sleep. Perhaps the Great Spirit will send us an answer in our dreams.'

In the morning they looked at each other hopefully.

'In my dream,' Deereeree began, 'I was on an island in the marsh. A tidal wave rolled in from the sea and flooded the lagoon. I stood on the highest part of the island, because that was all that was left of it, and as far as I could see there was water everywhere.'

'That's a lot of help!' Dinewan sneered. 'I dreamed I was on a flat plain and everywhere the birds and animals and snakes were fighting each other. They fought so long that none of them were left alive, and the plain was covered with bones. And that's just what will happen unless we do something about it,' he added savagely. 'Perhaps Kangaroo had a wonderful dream that will tell us what to do about it?'

'No, I had no dream, Dinewan. All night I lay awake. I kept thinking about a bone I found yesterday. It may well be that Baiame has put this thought in me for a purpose. Let us go and look at it.'

The two birds followed Kangaroo to the place where the bone was lying on the ground. Emu dug with his strong claws and uncovered other bones. They were all pointing in the same direction.

'There is a reason for this,' Deereeree twittered.

'Then tell us what it is,' croaked Dinewan.

Mirram picked up the bone he had first discovered.

'There is magic in it,' he shouted excitedly. 'I can feel it inside me.'

He dug one end of the bone into the ground and pushed against it. It moved of its own accord, with Mirram holding on to one end and the birds running after him. It followed the direction in which the other bones were pointing, leaving a deep trench behind it. There was a sudden roar, and when the friends looked back they saw white-capped waves and a torrent of water rushing down the channel that the bone had made.

'This is the tidal wave I saw in my dream,' cried Deereeree.

The three friends ran faster, and the water raced behind them, filling the trench, spilling into the marsh lands, flooding the lagoons until they overflowed, and all the trees and rushes were submerged. The lizards and animals fled to dry land as fast as their legs would carry them. The birds rose up in a vast cloud and flew from their homes. By nightfall not a single bird or animal was to be seen. The fertile marshes lay underneath a single sheet of water, stretching right out to the horizon.